Architektur und Raum
Gestaltungskonzepte im
20. Jahrhundert

Architecture and Space
Design Concepts in the
20th Century

Architektur und Raum
Gestaltungskonzepte im
20. Jahrhundert

Egon Schirmbeck / Till Boettger / Christian Hanke

Architecture and Space
Design Concepts in the
20th Century

Egon Schirmbeck / Till Boettger / Christian Hanke

Inhalt

Egon Schirmbeck, Till Boettger	Vorwort __ 6
Egon Schirmbeck	*Raum'Gestalt* __ 10
	Zur Analyse von Raumkonzepten __ 16
Frank Lloyd Wright	Unity Temple, 1907 __ 30
Frank Lloyd Wright	Haus für Frederick C. Robie, 1910 __ 36
Robert van 't Hoff	Villa Henny, 1919 __ 42
Theo van Doesburg, Cornelis van Eesteren	Maison Particulière, 1923 __ 48
Gerrit T. Rietveld	Haus Schröder, 1924 __ 54
Le Corbusier	Pavillon de L'Esprit Nouveau, 1925 __ 60
Walter Gropius	Meisterhaus Feininger, 1926 __ 66
Hans Scharoun	Haus 33, Weißenhofsiedlung, 1927 __ 72
Theo van Doesburg	Café de l'Aubette, 1928 __ 78
Ludwig Mies van der Rohe	Barcelona-Pavillon, 1929 __ 84
Le Corbusier	Villa Savoye, 1931 __ 90
Frank Lloyd Wright	Haus E. J. Kaufmann, Fallingwater, 1939 __ 96
Charles & Ray Eames	Eames House, 1949 __ 102
Le Corbusier	Chapelle Notre-Dame-du-Haut, 1954 __ 108
Carlo Scarpa	Olivetti Showroom, 1958 __ 114
Robert Venturi	Haus für Vanna Venturi, 1964 __ 120
Herman Hertzberger	Centraal Beheer, 1972 __ 126
Mario Botta	Casa Bianchi, 1973 __ 132
Mario Campi, Franco Pessina	Casa Felder, 1973 __ 138
Louis I. Kahn	Yale Center for British Art, 1977 __ 144
Tadao Ando	Haus Koshino, 1981 __ 150
Christian de Portzamparc	Café Beaubourg, 1986 __ 156
Günther Domenig	Steinhaus, 1986 __ 162
Zaha Hadid	Werksfeuerwehr, 1993 __ 168
Peter Zumthor	Therme Vals, 1996 __ 174
UN-Studio van Berkel & Bos	Möbius-Haus, 1998 __ 180
Axel Schultes, Charlotte Frank	Krematorium, 1998 __ 186
Rem Koolhaas	Maison à Bordeaux, 1998 __ 192
William Alsop	Peckham Library, 1999 __ 198
Peter Zumthor	Schweizer Pavillon, 2000 __ 204
Frank O. Gehry	DZ Bank AG, 2001 __ 210
	Register __ 216

Contents

Egon Schirmbeck, Till Boettger — Preface __ 6

Egon Schirmbeck — *Raum'Gestalt* __ 10
On the analysis of spatial concepts __ 16

Frank Lloyd Wright	Unity Temple, 1907 __ 30
Frank Lloyd Wright	Frederick C. Robie House, 1910 __ 36
Robert van 't Hoff	Villa Henny, 1919 __ 42
Theo van Doesburg, Cornelis van Eesteren	Maison Particulière, 1923 __ 48
Gerrit T. Rietveld	Schroeder House, 1924 __ 54
Le Corbusier	Pavillon de L'Esprit Nouveau, 1925 __ 60
Walter Gropius	Meisterhaus Feininger, 1926 __ 66
Hans Scharoun	House 33, Weißenhofsiedlung, 1927 __ 72
Theo van Doesburg	Café de l'Aubette, 1928 __ 78
Ludwig Mies van der Rohe	Barcelona-Pavillon, 1929 __ 84
Le Corbusier	Villa Savoye, 1931 __ 90
Frank Lloyd Wright	E. J. Kaufmann House, Fallingwater, 1939 __ 96
Charles & Ray Eames	Eames House, 1949 __ 102
Le Corbusier	Chapelle Notre-Dame-du-Haut, 1954 __ 108
Carlo Scarpa	Olivetti Showroom, 1958 __ 114
Robert Venturi	House for Vanna Venturi, 1964 __ 120
Herman Hertzberger	Centraal Beheer, 1972 __ 126
Mario Botta	Casa Bianchi, 1973 __ 132
Mario Campi, Franco Pessina	Casa Felder, 1973 __ 138
Louis I. Kahn	Yale Center for British Art, 1977 __ 144
Tadao Ando	Koshino House, 1981 __ 150
Christian de Portzamparc	Café Beaubourg, 1986 __ 156
Günther Domenig	Steinhaus, 1986 __ 162
Zaha Hadid	Vitra Fire Station, 1993 __ 168
Peter Zumthor	Therme Vals, 1996 __ 174
UN-Studio van Berkel & Bos	Moebius House, 1998 __ 180
Axel Schultes, Charlotte Frank	Krematorium, 1998 __ 186
Rem Koolhaas	Maison à Bordeaux, 1998 __ 192
William Alsop	Peckham Library, 1999 __ 198
Peter Zumthor	Schweizer Pavillon, 2000 __ 204
Frank O. Gehry	DZ Bank AG, 2001 __ 210

Index __ 218

Vorwort

Im Fach Entwerfen an der Bauhaus-Universität Weimar werden im Bachelor-Studiengang die Grundbegriffe des räumlichen Gestaltens vermittelt. In Vorlesungen und Übungen werden wesentliche Entwurfs- und Gestaltungsparameter räumlicher Zusammenhänge unterschiedlicher Nutzungs- und Funktionsbereiche erarbeitet. In Verbindung mit Seminaren zum Raum in der Architektur und zu Theorien zum Raum, Seminaren zur Darstellung von Zusammenhängen zwischen Raum und Form, zu Prinzipien der Raumgestaltung sollen die Studierenden durch Wahrnehmungsübungen räumliche Situationen und deren gestalterische Beziehung zueinander erkennen. Es wird versucht, die wesentlichen Gestaltungskonzepte – wie zum Beispiel das Konzept der Wege oder der Lichtführung durch die Wechselwirkungen zwischen Raum, Material, Farbe und Textur sowie Einrichtungselemente – anhand der Architekturen zu erkennen. In einem eigenen Entwurfsprojekt werden anschließend die neuen Erfahrungen umgesetzt. Die didaktische Struktur verfolgt in einem ersten Schritt die Analyse von Entwurfs- und Gestaltungsparametern von Räumen. In einem zweiten Schritt erfolgt die Synthese einzelner Parameter.

In der ersten Aufgabe werden die Elemente der Raumbildung und deren gestalterische Zusammenhänge durch die Analyse von konkreten räumlichen Situationen studiert. In der zweiten Aufgabe wird nach den Analysen ein eigenes Entwurfsprojekt angefertigt. Jedes der Analysebeispiele ist durch ein Charakteristikum seines materiellen, räumlich-gestalterischen Gefüges geprägt. Je nach Projekt und in Abhängigkeit des zur Verfügung stehenden Quellen- und Informationsmaterials werden folgende Parameter herausgearbeitet:

Preface

Design courses in the Bachelor's degree program at Bauhaus University Weimar teach the basic concepts of spatial design. Fundamental design and construction parameters for various functional areas are developed in lectures and tutorials. In conjunction with introductions to the concept of space in architecture, to theories of space, to the depiction of interrelationships between space and form and to principles of spatial design, perceptual exercises and experiments are designed to enable students to recognize spatial conditions and their creative interconnections. With the help of various architectural examples, students develop their ability to recognize fundamental design concepts, such as those of paths or lighting, through the interplay of space, material, color and texture as well as furnishings. Students then design their own project, in which they synthesize and implement the experience and knowledge they have gathered. The didactic structure consists firstly of a stage in which design and construction parameters for spaces are analyzed. In a second step, individual parameters are synthesized.

In the first task, the elements of spatial design and their creative interconnections are studied through the analysis of concrete spatial conditions. Following this preparation, students use the knowledge and experience gained from the analyses in a design project of their own. Each example to be analyzed is characterized by a particular aspect of its physico-spatial structure. In accordance with the individual projects and depending on the source material and additional information available, the following parameters are established:

A Raumgestalt: Material, Farbe, Licht
B Raumfunktion: Raum und Nutzung
C Raumbildung: Körper und Raum
D Raumstruktur: Form und Ordnung
E Raumfolge: Orte und Wege

Als Anschauungsbeispiele werden herausragende und exemplarische Gebäude, Räume bzw. Gestaltungskonzepte, im Allgemeinen des 20. und 21. Jahrhunderts, analysiert. Diesen Objekten liegen programmatische Gestaltungsabsichten zugrunde, die durch diese geistige Begegnung im Sinne einer Wahrnehmungsübung sichtbar gemacht werden können.

Ergänzend zu dieser zweidimensionalen Betrachtungsweise werden in einem Modell zusätzlich »reale« räumliche Zusammenhänge visualisiert. Auf diese Weise wird versucht, das räumliche Konzept der Analyseobjekte aufzuspüren und dieses zu verdichten. Als Vertiefung wird von den Studierenden auf Grundlage der Raumanalysen ein Lindenholzmodell im Maßstab 1:33 1/3 geplant und angefertigt. Der Bühnenbildmaßstab als auch die Selektion des Ausschnitts sollen helfen, die räumlichen Zusammenhänge so darzustellen, dass der architektonische Raum im Modell wahrnehmbar und nachvollziehbar wird. Im Prozess dieses Modellbaus wird die Abstraktion der Analyse genutzt, um die für das Architekturbeispiel wesentlichen Raumparameter darzustellen. Es wird bewusst weitgehend auf Farbe und zusätzliche Materialien neben dem Lindenholz im Modellbau verzichtet, um die Raumkonzepte in ihrer Essenz zu zeigen. Die Konzentration auf die wesentlichen architektonischen Entwurfswerkzeuge, nämlich Zeichnung und physisches Modell, soll genutzt

A Spatial design: Material, color, light
B Spatial function: Space and use
C Spatial definition: Objects and space
D Spatial structure: Form and order
E Spatial sequence: Places and paths

The examples to be analyzed are outstanding and exemplary buildings, spaces and design concepts – generally from the 20th and 21st centuries. Underlying many of these objects are architectural agendas which can be revealed through an intellectual encounter in the form of perceptual exercises.

In addition to these 2-dimensional approaches, models are used to facilitate the visualization of "real" spatial interconnections. These models attempt to detect and intensify the spatial concepts found in the examples. In order to deepen their understanding, students plan and construct a limewood model on a scale of 1.33 1/3 based on spatial analysis. Both the required stage scale and the selection of a section are designed to help present the spatial interconnections in such a way that architectural space becomes perceptible and comprehensible. The model-building process utilizes the abstraction of analysis to present the spatial parameters that are at the core of the architectural example. The models generally do without the use of color or of materials other than limewood, so that spatial concepts can be shown in their essence. The students are thus given an opportunity to immerse themselves in the spatial design of outstanding architectures. Concentration on the central design tools of

werden, um den Studierenden ein architektonisches Vokabular zu vermitteln. In der Diskussion am konkreten Beispiel können Begriffe geübt, der Vorstellungsraum erweitert und das Lesen der architektonischen Haltung versucht werden. Indem der Fokus der Studierenden auf jeweils ein Gebäude gelegt wird, sollen die Zusammenhänge der Raumparameter sichtbar gemacht und dadurch das Lesen und das Schreiben von Architektur begreifbar gelehrt werden.

Für diese Dokumentation wurden unterschiedliche Studien- bzw. Analyseobjekte der vergangenen Studienjahre ausgewählt. Im Hinblick auf das Tätigkeitsfeld des Architekten – die Realisierung von nutzbaren Räumen – ist auch diese Auswahl nicht vollständig. Zur Erzeugung eines vertiefenden Bewusstseins für räumliche Zusammenhänge kann die »Raumbibliothek« beliebig »weitergebaut« werden. Gleichzeitig können damit auch Strömungen, Tendenzen und einzelne Entwicklungslinien in der Gestaltung von Räumen im 20. und 21. Jahrhundert sichtbar gemacht werden. In dieser Publikation wird versucht, den Zusammenhang der wesentlichen Entwurfsparameter aufzuzeigen und nachvollziehbar zu machen. Sowohl die Fotos der physischen Modelle als auch die Raumanalysen sollen nicht die realen Architekturen abbilden, sondern räumliche Situationen darstellen, die man nicht real erleben kann. Die räumlichen und grafischen Analysen ermöglichen einen neuen Blick auf die Architektur.

Wir hoffen, mit dieser Dokumentation dazu beizutragen, die komplexen Schichten der Raumgestaltung bei unterschiedlichen Konzepten sichtbar zu machen.

architecture, namely drafting and physical models, serves to provide students with the vocabulary of architecture. While discussing concrete examples, students can practise terminology, expand their capacity for visualizing and try their hand at interpreting architectural approaches. By focusing on one building at a time, students should recognize the interconnections between spatial parameters, and the reading and writing of architecture should be made comprehensible to them.

Various representative objects for analysis that have been used in past years were chosen for the documentation at hand. Given the task of architects – the realization of usable spaces – this selection cannot be comprehensive or complete. This "spatial library" can be extended and additions can be "built" to facilitate a deeper awareness of spatial interconnections. At the same time, movements, trends and individual lines of development in 20th- and 21st-century design can be traced. This publication seeks to illustrate the relationships between the fundamental design parameters and to make these comprehensible. Neither the photos of the physical models nor the spatial analyses are meant to depict the actual architectural objects, but should rather present spatial conditions that one is not able to experience in real life. Hence the spatial and graphical analyses attempt to provide a new view of architecture.

We hope that this publication will help to reveal the complex layers of spatial design under the influence of various concepts.

Für die Unterstützung unseres Projekts möchten wir uns sehr bei unseren Förderern bedanken, ohne deren Engagement und Verständnis für die Raumgestaltung wäre diese Publikation nicht möglich gewesen. Mit der Gestaltung der verschiedenen Elemente haben sie erheblichen Einfluss auf die Inszenierung der erlebbaren Räume.

Des Weiteren möchten wir uns bei Sophie Gläser für die Geduld, das große Engagement und die sensible Kreativität bei der Umsetzung dieser Publikation bedanken.

Egon Schirmbeck, Till Boettger

We would like to thank our sponsors for their tremendous support with our project. This publication would not have been possible without their commitment and their understanding of spatial design. Through their design of the various elements, they had a significant influence on the staging of the spatial experiences.

We would also like to thank Sophie Gläser for her patience, her dedication and her caring creativity in realizing this publication project.

Egon Schirmbeck, Till Boettger

Egon Schirmbeck *Raum'Gestalt*

Im Durchschnitt hält sich der Mensch – je nach Kulturraum und Beruf – etwa 95 Prozent seiner Lebenszeit in Räumen, respektive Innenräumen auf (neben dem Naturraum oder Stadtraum oder Luftraum – einige auch im Weltraum). Räume, in denen wir wohnen und arbeiten, Räume der Erholung (Kino, Sportstätten, Theater) oder Therapie (Klinik), Forschung und Lehre oder Räume für die Kunst bzw. Ausstellungsräume.

Jeder weiß aus eigener Erfahrung, dass ein Raum bzw. dessen Geometrie (Höhe / Länge / Breite), seine Materialbeschaffenheit (harte oder weiche Materialien mit Auswirkungen auf die Akustik – zum Beispiel »schallweiche Räume«) oder seine Farbtemperatur (»kalte« oder »warme« Räume) alle menschlichen Sinne anspricht. Im Unterbewusstsein registrieren wir vorn und hinten, suchen das Geborgene und den geschützten Rücken (seitliches Umgehen der Vierung in der Kirche / Sitzen im Restaurant an der Wand). Der dunkle Raum (oder auch der Wald) kann Ängste hervorrufen, unser Geruchssinn kann zum Beispiel durch Äther in der Klinik ebenfalls Ängste bewirken oder er kann zur Appetitlosigkeit führen (Mensaduft / Restaurant). Zugang durch spezielle Gestaltsituation – Schwellenangst – öffnen oder schließen.

In der Geschichte der Architektur zeigt sich immer wieder die herausragende Bedeutung der Inszenierung von Räumen: Kulträume im alten Ägypten (Raumfolgen einzelner Hofsequenzen), in der Antike (raffinierte Erschließungswege) oder die spannenden Raumfolgen christlicher Sakralräume – Rauminszenierung aber auch zur Manipulation unserer Gefühle: Hier vor der Tür ein Paradebeispiel (im wahrsten Sinne des Wortes) zur Inszenierung von Macht: das Gauforum – gesteigert beim Zeppelinfeld in Nürnberg – das Individuum verschwindet in der Masse und Größe. Diese

Egon Schirmbeck *Raum'Gestalt*

Approximately 95 per cent of the average person's life, depending on his or her culture and occupation, is spent in rooms, or to be more exact, interior spaces (as opposed to nature or urban spaces or airspace – in some cases even outer space): rooms in which we live and work, recreational (cinema, sport facility, theatre), therapeutic (clinic), research and educational spaces, or art and exhibition spaces.

We have all experienced how a room and its geometry (height / length / width), its material characteristics (hard or soft materials with effects on acoustics – for example rooms with acoustically permeable walls) or its color temperature ("cold" or "warm" rooms) stimulate all our human senses. We subconsciously register where the front and the back of a room are; we seek out security and protect our own backs (avoiding the crossing in a church, sitting next to a wall in a restaurant). A dark room – or the forest – can induce fears; our sense of smell can, influenced by the smell of ether in a clinic, for example, also provoke fears or dull our appetites (here canteen smells / a restaurant). Access by virtue of a special *gestalt* situation – fear of crossing a threshold – opening or closing.

The history of architecture is actually full of examples of the extraordinary importance of staging space(s): cult chambers in ancient Egypt (with their series of courtyards), in ancient Greece and Rome (clever approaches) or the thrill of room sequences in Christian places of worship. But space staging to manipulate our emotions as well: right in front of our door here in Weimar a prime example (the German expression *Paradebeispiel* (parade

Inszenierung von »Machträumen« bewog Hans Scharoun bei seiner Philharmonie – geradezu als Reflex –, dem Individuum wieder seinen eigenen, maßstäblichen Raum zurückzugeben: Die Gliederung in kleine und überschaubare, locker gruppierte Sitzzonen, unterschiedlich in ihrer Ausformung, möglicherweise auch als Synonym einer neuen, heterogenen demokratischen Gesellschaft.

Die Konzeption, Entwicklung und Realisierung von nutzbaren Räumen ist das zentrale Tätigkeitsfeld des Architekten: Dies beginnt bei der Struktur und Gestaltung von Stadträumen und deren Verknüpfung mit dem Naturraum (»Erholungsraum«), der Organisation unterschiedlicher Raumsequenzen innerhalb eines Gebäudes (in der DIN reduziert auf Verkehrs-/ Nutzflächen – oder besser Weg-/ Ortsräume) und führt schließlich zur Form und Gestalt eines einzelnen Raums – ein Gebilde, das nach Laotse gar nicht fassbar ist, sondern ausschließlich durch seine raumbegrenzenden Elemente (also Wände, Decke, Fußboden) entsprechende Empfindungen bei uns auslösen kann.

Heinrich Zille sagte sinngemäß: Man kann einen Menschen mit seiner Wohnung erschlagen. »Jemand platzt herein« oder »mit der Türe ins Haus fallen« sind Zustandsbeschreibungen negativer räumlicher Situationen bzw. Beschreibungen über die Behandlung von Räumen. Es ist noch unbekannt, warum in den letzten Jahrzehnten die Farbe Weiß im Innenraum eindeutig vorherrscht. Möglicherweise zur Schaffung einer neutralen Umgebung, als Angebot zur Selbstinszenierung oder als Antwort auf den Einsatz moderner Heizungssysteme. Jetzt ist es nicht mehr nötig, die Wohnung mit »warmen« Farbtönen »optisch aufzuheizen«. Umgekehrt wurde nachgewiesen, dass bei sogenannten warmen Farben die

example) is doubly appropriate) for the staging of power – the "Gauforum" – intensified in the Zeppelin Field in Nuremberg – the individual disappears within the sheer mass and size. Such staging of "power dreams" led the German architect Hans Scharoun in his Berliner Philharmonie – almost as a reflex – to give back to the individual his own scale of space: its ordering into small and manageable loosely-grouped sitting areas and: varying in shape – perhaps as a synonym for a new, heterogeneous democratic society.

Designing, developing and implementing – usable – spaces is the central set of tasks for an architect: this begins with the structure and design of the urban environment and its links to the surrounding natural spaces ("recreation areas"), the organization of a wide range of room sequences within a building (reduced to traffic areas versus utilizable areas – or rather paths and spaces – in the German *DIN standards*) and in the end leads to the shape and configuration of a single room. An entity that, according to Laozi, cannot be comprehended but rather can invoke sensations in us purely through its space-defining elements (namely walls, ceiling, floor).

Heinrich Zille said (in reference to tenement housing in Berlin): "You can kill someone with an axe, but you can also slay him with an apartment." To "climb the walls" or "barge in" are descriptions of – negative – experiences of rooms or our dealings with them. It is still unclear why in the last decades the color white has been so dominant in interior decorating – perhaps as a neutral environment for our self-presentations or due to perfect heating systems that make "warm" tones superfluous – conversely, with

tatsächliche Raumtemperatur um ein bis zwei Grad reduziert werden kann. Gleichzeitig hat ein anderes Medium der Gebäudetechnik dazu geführt, dass wir das Phänomen der Dämmerung kaum noch erfahren. Es geht nur noch um hell oder dunkel: Licht an oder aus.

Für Louis Kahn war die natürliche Belichtung mit dem Farbspektrum des Tagesablaufs ein zentraler Entwurfs- und Gestaltungsparameter. Mit großem technischen bzw. hohem Energieaufwand versucht die japanische Kaufhauskette Mitsukoshi, die Kauflust durch eine konstante Beleuchtung, orientiert am Tageslichtspektrum, zu steigern. Im Kaufhaus wird unsere unbewusste räumliche Orientierung und Wahrnehmung geschickt zur Steigerung der Umsatzraten – manipuliert: Der Mensch neigt im Allgemeinen dazu, sich im Raum nach rechts zu orientieren (empirische Studien). Diese Erkenntnis führt uns im Erdgeschoss – meist nach rechts – vorzugsweise direkt in die Strumpf- und Sockenabteilung – die Abteilung in einem Kaufhaus mit der höchsten Umsatzrendite!

Diese wenigen Beispiele zeigen bereits die breite Bedeutung der Entwicklung von räumlichen Sequenzen und deren Einfluss auf unser Bewusstsein und Wohlbefinden.

In den Diskussionen um Effizienz oder die Erfüllung von Energieeinsparfaktoren in der Energieeinsparverordnung (EnEV) gehen die Bedürfnisse nach dem »Lebensmittel« der Raumqualität schnell unter. Erst kürzlich in einer Jury für einen Kindergarten: In der Auslobung war kein Hinweis oder gar eine Forderung für besondere Raumqualitäten als pädagogisches Gestaltungskonzept. Der Kindergarten heißt auch noch *Friedrich Fröbel*. Apropos Wettbewerbe: Heute werden

so-called warm colors we can reduce the actual room temperature by one or two degrees. At the same time, through another building technology medium, the light switch, we hardly experience dawn or dusk any more (it's all a matter of bright or dark).

For Louis Kahn, natural light in the color spectrum of an average day was a fundamental design and construction parameter. The Japanese department store chain Mitsukoshi has invested a great deal of technology and energy in lighting which mimics daylight in order to raise customers' inclination to buy. Department stores cleverly manipulate our subconscious spatial orientation and perception in order to increase turnover. People tend to orient themselves to the right in space (empirical studies). This insight leads us – usually to the right – preferably into the hosiery section – the department with the highest return on sales of a typical department store.

These selected examples show the wide significance of designed spatial sequences and their influence on our consciousness and feeling of well-being.

In discussions regarding efficiency or attention to energy-saving factors in the German regulation for energy saving in buildings and building systems (*Energieeinsparverordnung – EnEV*), the need for the "sustenance" of room quality is easily forgotten – seldom is it "commissioned" by the client. Recently, in a jury for a kindergarten project: The competition included no mention of, to say nothing of a requirement for, a particular spatial quality as a pedagogical design concept, although the kindergarten in question is to bear the name *Friedrich Fröbel*. On the topic

Wettbewerbe und sogenannte Verhandlungsverfahren mit ausgetüftelten Kriterien der Zulassung ausgelobt. Absolventen und Anfänger haben kaum Chancen, ihre kreativen Fähigkeiten einer zeitgenössischen Raumgestaltung zu präsentieren, geschweige denn zu realisieren: Abgefragt werden Umsatzvolumen, Zahl der Mitarbeiter, Jahre der Berufserfahrung – ohne nicht schon fünf Kindergärten gebaut zu haben, keine Zulassung. Zur Erinnerung: Meinhard von Gerkan und Volkwin Marg haben als Studenten den Wettbewerb für den Flughafen Tegel gewonnen; Ludwig Mies van der Rohe hätte heutzutage niemals die Weißenhofsiedlung in Stuttgart planen können.

Dabei ist Erfahrung relativ – mit Tucholsky: »Man kann eine Sache auch 35 Jahre falsch machen.«

Raum'Gestalt – Thema der Ausstellung des Lehrstuhls Entwerfen und Innenraumgestaltung der Bauhaus-Universität Weimar im vergangenen Jahr – als ein zentrales Tätigkeitsfeld der Architekten. Zur Annäherung an diesen komplexen Verantwortungsbereich versuchen wir an unserem Lehrstuhl, in Seminaren und Übungen besondere, wegweisende und vor allem qualitativ hochwertige Raumgestaltungskonzepte, das heißt einzelne Entwurfsparameter, zu analysieren. Mit der zeichnerischen Analyse im Sinne einer Deduktion – als Ableitung des Besonderen, Erkenntnis des Einzelfalls – wird die Entwurfskonzeption bis in ihre Einzelteile zurückverfolgt. Einzelne Entwurfsparameter werden zeichnerisch herausgelöst. Bei dieser Betrachtungsweise wird der Entwurf in seine raumkonstituierenden und gestaltprägenden Elemente zerlegt und dadurch sichtbar gemacht. Die Analyse ist – didaktisch gesehen – die Grundlage für die Synthese in den anschließenden Entwurfsübungen. Ergänzend zur

of competitions: Nowadays competitions and so-called negotiation processes are held with carefully developed criteria for permission to participate. Graduates and novices have next to no chance of presenting their fresh, creative abilities in contemporary spatial design, to say nothing of realizing them. The criteria are turnover, number of employees, years of experience – if you haven't built at least five kindergartens don't even bother applying – a reminder: Meinhard von Gerkan and Volkwin Marg won the Tegel airport competition when they were students / Ludwig Mies van der Rohe would never have been able to plan the Weißenhofsiedlung in Stuttgart.

But experience is relative – as Tucholsky says: "35 years can also be spent doing something badly."

Raum'Gestalt – the theme of the exhibition of Bauhaus University Weimar – as a central architectural field of activity. Our department aims to approach this complex area of responsibility through the analysis, in seminars and tutorials, of outstanding, seminal and most importantly high-quality spatial design concepts, that is, to investigate individual design parameters. Using graphical analysis in the sense of a deduction – filtering out what is extraordinary, recognizing individual cases / with regard to design: the design concept is traced back to its separate parts, particular design parameters are made explicit and shown individually in drawings. This approach helps to reveal and deconstruct the design into the elements with which it defines space and forms structures. From a didactic perspective, the analysis serves as a basis for the synthesis in the subsequent design tasks. In addition to two-dimensional visualizations, spatial, that means

zweidimensionalen Visualisierung werden räumliche, das heißt dreidimensionale Zusammenhänge, in einem Modell sichtbar gemacht. Im Modell sind wesentliche Elemente der abstrakten zweidimensionalen zeichnerischen Darstellung oder auch der sogenannten virtuellen Räume in einer proportional richtigen, räumlich-gestalterischen Gesamtheit sichtbar. Diese Lehrveranstaltungen fanden im Allgemeinen in den ersten Semestern (Diplom-Studiengang/Grundstudium oder jetzt Bachelor-Studiengang) statt, auch um die Studierenden bereits möglichst früh mit herausragenden und charakteristischen Architektur- und Raumkonzepten vertraut zu machen.

Auch diese Analysen sind nur Hilfsmittel, sich einer späteren Realität anzunähern. Denn Bauen ist ein physischer Prozess: Es geht um Konstruktionen, um Material, Licht, Dimensionen. Deshalb wäre es eigentlich besser: Studium vor Ort im Maßstab 1:1. Ziel: Studiengang Hälfte Theorie/Hälfte Studium vor Ort von herausragenden Raumkonzepten – mit Nutzern und Architekten.

Die neue Struktur mit Bachelor und Master lässt dies kaum zu. Auch wenn überall bzw. eigentlich von der Politik kolportiert wird, mehr in Bildung zu investieren, erfolgt bei dieser Studienstruktur eine Reduzierung in der Ausbildung. Gleichwohl – die Struktur ist an sich sinnvoll bezüglich der individuellen Möglichkeiten, Studieninhalte zu verfolgen. Die Studienpläne sind derzeit noch sehr kompliziert. Es bleibt die Hoffnung auf Deregulierung und auf die Schaffung von »Frei-Räumen« für freies Denken und die Hoffnung auf Ignoranz gegenüber dem erschreckenden Akkreditierungswahn der Akkreditierungsagenturen, die sich jedes Semester neue Geschäftsfelder zur Vergabe fragwürdiger Labels suchen.

three-dimensional interrelationships are made explicit in a model. The model reveals fundamental elements of the abstract two-dimensional graphic illustration or even so-called virtual rooms in their correctly proportioned spatially conceived entirety. These courses were generally included in the first semesters (Diploma or the current Bachelor's degree) in order to familiarize students as soon as possible with outstanding and representative architectural and spatial concepts.

These analyses are tools for approximating a future reality. Building is a physical process: it is a matter of constructions, of material/light/dimensions. What would really be better: studies on site on a scale of 1:1 – Goal: course of studies half theory/half on-site study of outstanding and high-quality spatial designs – with users and architects.

The new programs with Bachelor's and Master's degrees hardly allow for such approaches. Although calls to invest much more in education can be heard everywhere – or more exactly among politicians, the new structuring of courses of studies results in a narrowing of perspectives and reductions in the study of spatial design. Nonetheless – the new structure is sensible in and of itself with regard to its opportunities for individuals to investigate particular content areas. The curricula are still very complicated – we continue to hope for deregulation and the creation of "free spaces" for free thinking – and ignorance regarding the appalling "accreditation-itis" of the accreditation agencies and their search, each semester, for new markets in which they can award questionable labels.

Entsprechend der Erkenntnis von Phaidros möge diese Auseinandersetzung mit herausragenden Räumen des 20. Jahrhunderts dazu beitragen, das Bewusstsein der Zusammenhänge bei der Gestaltung von Räumen zu fördern.

»Sag mir (da du so empfänglich bist für die Wirkungen der Architektur),
hast du nicht beobachtet,
wenn du dich in dieser Stadt ergingst,
dass unter den Räumen (Bauwerken),
die sie ausmachen,
einige stumm sind,
andere reden,
und noch andere schließlich,
und das sind die seltensten,
singen sogar?« * [1]

* Phaidros zu Sokrates
   In: Valéry, Paul: *Eupalinos oder Der Architekt.* Paris 1923
   (*Eupalinous ou l'Architecte, précédé de l'Ame et la Danse.*)

[1] Vortrag zur Finissage der Ausstellung *Raum'Gestalt*
   im Neuen Museum Weimar, 2010 – gekürzte Fassung

Egon Schirmbeck *Zur Analyse von Raumkonzepten*

Der Ursprung einzelner Strömungen und Tendenzen der Architektur respektive von Raum- und Gestaltungskonzepten lässt sich im Allgemeinen auf meist wenige geistige Urheber zurückführen: Architekten, die zu bestimmten Zeiten für spezielle Bauaufgaben (Probleme) charakteristische Lösungen entwickelt und mit jeweils spezifischen baulichen Mitteln realisiert haben. Vitruv hat zum Beispiel seine Grundlagen und Prinzipien in zehn Büchern zusammengefasst, Palladio seine Gestaltungsprinzipien in vier Büchern festgehalten. Den Eleven der École Polytechnique in Paris wurde der Katalog einzelner Gebäudetypen von Durand zum Studium vorgegeben und Le Corbusier hat in zahlreichen Manifesten und Schriften einschließlich der *Charta von Athen* (mehrere Schlussredaktionen stammen von ihm) seine Prinzipien für eine neue Architektur im 20. Jahrhundert dargelegt.

Auch wenn noch immer gern das Image des kreativen Architekten, der angeblich Ursprüngliches, Authentisches kreiert, gepflegt wird, zeigt die Entwicklung bis heute auch, dass zu allen Zeiten auf die Erkenntnisse und Lösungsvorschläge einiger weniger Wegbereiter zurückgegriffen wurde. Zumal es ohnehin nicht sein kann, wie es Mies van der Rohe formuliert hat, dass jeden Montag eine neue Architektur erfunden wird. Damit allerdings nicht Formen ohne Inhalt entstehen, die zu unnötigen Missverständnissen führen (das nicht nutzbare Flachdach, der monotone weiße Kubus der Moderne, die oft simpel rezipierte neue Einfachheit), scheint es mir doch wichtig zu sein, die jeweiligen Prinzipien und Grundlagen der »geistigen Urheber« zu erkennen und zu verstehen, um diese für die eigenen, ähnlichen Probleme angemessen transformieren zu können. Gerade durch die Fülle von Raumkonzepten und Visionen, die im 20. Jahrhundert entstanden

Egon Schirmbeck *On the analysis of spatial concepts*

The origin of individual trends and tendencies in architecture, or rather spatial and design concepts, can generally be traced to a fairly limited number of initiators: architects who each at a particular time found a characteristic solution with specific structural means for a particular architectural task (problem). Vitruvius, for example, collected his fundamentals and principles in ten books, Palladio recorded his design principles in four books, the élèves at the École Polytechnique in Paris were required to study Durand's catalogue of types of buildings, and Le Corbusier set down his principles for a new 20th-century architecture in numerous manifestos and documents, including the Athens Charter (he was responsible for many of the final versions).

As much as we cultivate the image of the creative architect whose designs are apparently original and authentic, history shows that throughout the various eras – and right up to the present – people have fallen back on the insights and solutions of a few pioneers; to quote Mies van der Rohe: "I refuse to invent a new architecture every Monday morning." To prevent the emergence of forms without contents and the ensuing misunderstandings (the unusable flat roof, the monotonous white cube of modernity, the new simplicity that is so often perceived simplistically) it strikes me as important to recognize and understand the fundamental principles of the "originators" in order to be able to transfer and adapt these for one's own solutions to similar problems. Given the abundance of spatial concepts and visions that developed in the 20th century and appear with ever greater speeds in architecture journals – worldwide before construction begins and nowadays also on the Internet – it seems more important than ever to understand the fundamental principles of new and conceivably groundbreaking concepts.

und ständig mit zunehmender Geschwindigkeit in Journalen – weltweit noch vor Baubeginn oder heute bequem im Internet – abrufbar sind, erscheint es mehr denn je notwendig, Grundlagen und Prinzipien neuer und möglicherweise wegweisender Konzepte zu verstehen.

Die wechselvollen Metamorphosen des Raums und die wenigen in dieser Publikation gezeigten Prototypen einzelner Stationen zeigen deutlich, dass es wohl auch in Zukunft kein einheitliches Raum- und Gestaltungskonzept mehr geben wird, das eine ganze Epoche charakterisiert. Die Antworten auf zu lösende Probleme werden zunehmend differenziert sein. Diese Vielfalt und vor allem die Freiheit, unterschiedliche Wege gehen zu können, ist eine große Errungenschaft dieses Jahrhunderts. Ein Umfeld, das die Möglichkeit bietet, individuellen Bedürfnissen und wechselnden Anforderungen gerecht werden zu können.

In the analysis in our seminars and tutorials of outstanding and representative spatial design concepts – generally from the 20th century – we aim to separate out the individual design parameters. Furthermore, beginning in the second semester, we would like to familiarize our young colleagues in "Fundamentals of Design" with representative spatial design concepts in the history of architecture.

The varied metamorphoses of space and this small sample of prototypes of various milestones make it quite clear that the future is also no more likely to yield a uniform spatial design concept that characterizes an entire era. The solutions to problems will be more and more sophisticated and multiform. This diversity and above all the freedom to choose different paths is a huge achievement of the past century. An environment that makes it possible to satisfy individual needs and meet changing requirements.

Eduardo Samsó
Nick Havanna Disco, Barcelona, 1986

RAUMBILDUNG
Körper und Raum

Die Raumbildung zur Organisation einzelner Nutzungsbereiche wird neben funktionellen Bedürfnissen durch den Charakter eines Raums und durch die äußeren Bedingungen geprägt. Dabei beeinflusst das Verhältnis zwischen Innen und Außen den Aufbau des Raums. Die Ausrichtung und Orientierung innerer Raumbereiche wird durch die gewünschte Beziehung nach Außen bestimmt, um entsprechende Leistungsanforderungen erfüllen zu können.

Während des Entwurfsprozesses wird das Wechselspiel der Beurteilung von Funktion, Charakter und den Beziehungen Innen / Außen vorweggenommen. Das Erleben eines Raums wird durch den Architekt definiert und durch eine entsprechende Anordnung der raumbildenden Elemente formuliert.

SPATIAL DEFINITION
Objects and space

The creation of spaces to organize functional areas is shaped not only by functional needs but also through the character of the room and by external conditions. The relationship between interior and exterior influences the structure of the room. The orientation and arrangement of the interior spaces are determined by the desired connection to the outside, so that associated requirements can be fulfilled.

During the design process, the interplay of appraisals of function, character and the interior / exterior relationships is anticipated. How a room will be experienced is defined by the architect and formulated with a corresponding layout of space-defining elements.

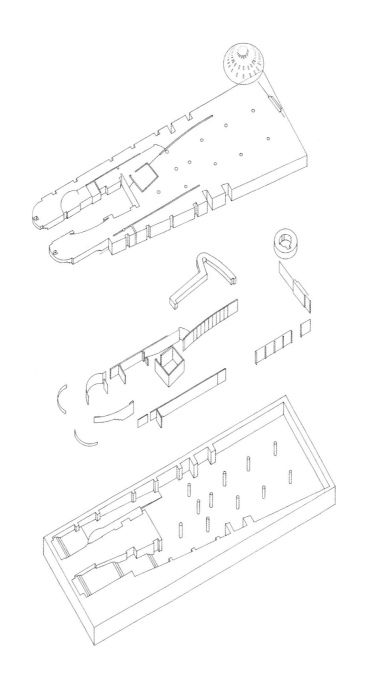

RAUMSTRUKTUR
Form und Ordnung

Das Ganze ist mehr als die Summe der Teile. Mit der Analyse der Raumstruktur wird das unsichtbare Netzwerk der Ordnung der Einzelteile in einem räumlichen Gesamtgefüge sichtbar. Ordnungsparameter wie Rasterstrukturen, Proportionen und Rhythmen prägen das Geflecht vernetzter Linien, nach denen vertikale und horizontale raumbegrenzende Elemente geordnet sind. Geometrische Prinzipien der Wiederholung, Teilung, Spiegelung, Rotation, Translation oder Addition sind innere Ordnungen zur Fügung des Ganzen.

Die Zuordnung von tragenden und nicht- Elementen, die geometrische Verflechtung der Raumteile oder die Abhängigkeit zwischen Innen und Außen können durch Teilbilder im Grund- und Aufriss oder in axonometrischen Raumbildern sichtbar gemacht werden. Die Analyse der Ordnungsstrukturen zeigt die übergeordnete Bedeutung geometrischer Konstruktionen für unterschiedliche Planungsebenen bzw. für die Durchgängigkeit einzelner Entwurfs- und Gestaltungsparameter vom großen bis zum kleinen Maßstab. Die Abhängigkeiten zwischen Form und Ordnung beschränken sich nicht nur auf konstruktive Zusammenhänge. Sie gelten auch für die Ordnung von Lichtstrukturen, Farb- und Materialtexturen oder für das Verhältnis von offenen zu geschlossenen Flächen und die Fügung von Baumaterialien.

SPATIAL STRUCTURE
Form and order

The whole is more than the sum of its parts. Analyzing spatial structure reveals the otherwise invisible network of the ordering of individual elements in a spatial structural whole. Order parameters such as grid structures, proportions and rhythms inform the mesh of interconnected lines by which the vertical and horizontal space-enclosing elements are arranged. Geometric principles of repetition, division, mirroring, translation or addition are inner orderings that bond the whole.

The assignment of load-bearing and non-load-bearing elements, the geometric meshing of individual room sections or the interdependence of interior and exterior can be shown with partial drawings in ground plans and elevations or in axonometric images. The analysis of individual structures also shows the primary significance of geometric constructions for the various planning levels and / or for consistency among design and construction parameters from large to small scales. Yet the interdependence between form and order is not limited to structural interconnections but also extends to the ordering of light structures, color and material textures or to the proportions of open to closed areas or the blending of construction materials.

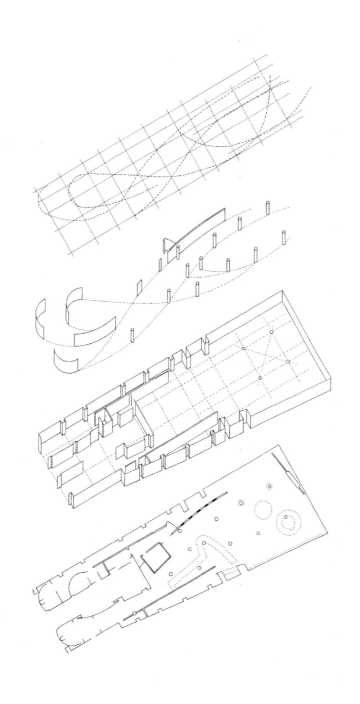

RAUMFOLGE
Orte und Wege

Die Folge von wechselnden Raumsequenzen kann dazu beitragen, ein Raumerlebnis zu vermitteln. Durch den räumlichen Aufbau können die Bewegungen im Raum gesteuert, differenziert und für besondere Nutzungen inszeniert werden. Die Art der Bewegung und die Atmosphäre der Raumsituation in der Realität sind in Abhängigkeit zu den funktionellen Entwurfsabsichten im Entwurf zu definieren.

Das Beziehungsnetz von Wegen kann aus Zonen der relativen Bewegungsruhe – Orträumen – und der gerichteten Bewegungsführung – Wegräumen – bestehen. Während der Ortraum bezüglich der Bewegungsintensität durch eine Ambivalenz gekennzeichnet ist, ist der Wegraum durch eine Konzentration auf ein Ziel und durch Bewegungsfrequenz geprägt. Horizontale Differenzierungen (Stufen, Rampen, Deckenvorsprünge) und Lichtinszenierungen oder Materialtexturen können zur Intensivierung eingesetzt werden.

Das Prinzip der Wegführung und die Hierarchie von Orten und Wegen ist ein zentrales Thema der Raumgestaltung. Bei Museen, Ausstellungen oder öffentlichen Gebäuden steht zum Beispiel die Auseinandersetzung mit der Bewegung im Raum häufig im Mittelpunkt der Entwurfskonzeption.

SPATIAL SEQUENCE
Places and paths

A set of changing spatial sequences can help to facilitate a particular experience of space. The ordering of space serves to channel and differentiate movement in a room and to stage it for particular utilization. The design should already define the nature of the movement and the atmosphere of the spatial conditions in reality, based on the corresponding functional design purposes.

The network of paths can be composed of relatively static zones – the "place spaces" – and those with a given traffic flow – the "path spaces". Place spaces have an ambivalent relationship to intensity of movement while path spaces are characterized by their focus on a goal or on connecting two places and by increasing frequency of motion. This intensity can be further increased through horizontal differentiation, for example steps or ramps or partially lowered ceilings, and lighting design or material textures.

The principle of traffic patterns and the hierarchy of places and paths is a central aspect of spatial design in numerous architectural projects. In museums, exhibitions or public buildings, for example, movement in space is often the main focus of the design concept.

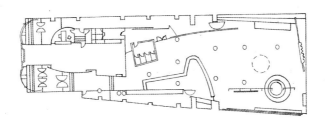

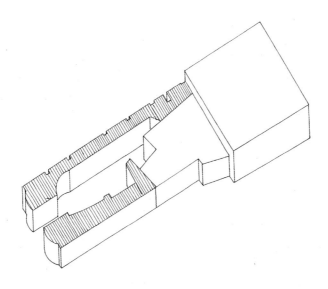

RAUMGESTALT
Material, Farbe, Licht

Die Atmosphäre, der Charakter und die Benutzbarkeit eines Raums werden wesentlich durch die Art und Weise der Beschaffenheit der Oberflächen der raumbegrenzenden Elemente bestimmt. Die Textur und Farbe der Materialien und deren Kombination prägen den räumlichen Ausdruck. Die Art und Weise der künstlichen und / oder natürlichen Belichtung beeinflusst die Reflektion und damit die wahrnehmbare Ausstrahlung der Oberflächen. Neben der Anordnung und der geometrischen Form sind oft wenige Millimeter der Oberflächenschicht von raumbildenden Elementen für das visuelle Erscheinungsbild und damit für die Ausstrahlung bzw. für eine wahrnehmbare Atmosphäre entscheidend.

Der Lichtführung und der Reflektion des Lichts durch unterschiedliche Texturen und Farbwerte der raumbegrenzenden Elemente kommt eine zentrale Bedeutung zur Erzeugung von Raumerlebnissen zu. Durch bewussten Einsatz von Material- und Farbkonstellationen in Verbindung mit unterschiedlichen Lichtquellen werden Abhängigkeiten und Wertigkeiten thematisiert. Auch können Zusammenhänge mit anderen Entwurfsparametern dargestellt werden.

SPATIAL DESIGN
Material, color, light

The atmosphere, character and usability of a room are largely determined by, along with other design parameters, the nature of the surfaces of its space-defining elements. The texture and color of materials, taken singly or together, shape the expression of the room and influence our perception of it. The nature of the artificial and / or natural lighting has an additional effect on reflection properties and hence how we perceive surfaces. Along with the arrangement and geometric forms of space-defining elements, often only a few millimeters in their surface layers can be of decisive importance for their appearance and thus their effect, that is to say for a perceptible atmosphere.

Light distribution and reflection through different textures and color values on the space-defining elements is centrally important in achieving particular spatial experiences for varying functional requirements. Deliberate use of material and color combinations in conjunction with varying light sources highlights interdependencies and valences within the spatial whole. In addition, correlations with other design parameters can be demonstrated.

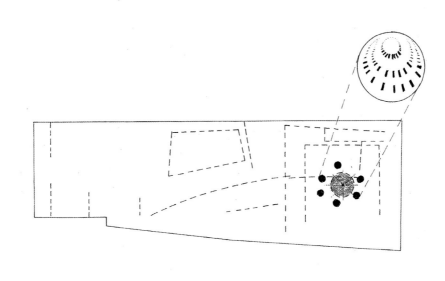

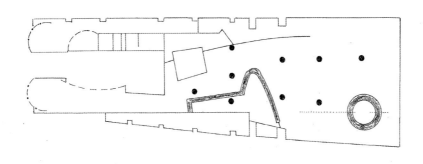

RAUMFUNKTION
Raum und Nutzung

Im Allgemeinen ermöglichen erst eingestellte mobile Elemente, Möbel oder Beleuchtungskörper die einem Raum zugedachte Nutzung und Funktion. Solche Elemente beeinflussen abschließend die räumliche Gliederung und Atmosphäre. Form, Größe, Material oder besondere Funktionsanforderungen dieser mobilen Einbauten bestimmen ihre Lage im Raum und ihre Beziehung zum Nutzer.

Die Funktionsbereiche innerhalb eines Raums werden durch die Anordnung und die Ausformung der raumbegrenzenden Elemente definiert. Zur Formulierung von einzelnen Funktionszonen können neben den vertikalen Raumbegrenzungen wie Wände oder Einbauelemente in besonderem Maße auch die horizontalen Raumabschlüsse wie Decke und Fußboden einbezogen werden. Bereits geringe Höhenversätze ermöglichen den Überblick über niedrige Raumzonen und bewirken so eine Begrenzung der Fläche bzw. definieren neue Raumzonen. Das Wechselspiel zwischen hohen und niedrigen Raumzonen führt zu einer Differenzierung der Raumbereiche und trägt zu wechselnden Raumfolgen bei.

SPATIAL FUNCTION
Space and use

In general, a room can only fulfill its planned use and function with the inclusion of movable elements, furniture or lights. Such elements, in turn, influence the spatial arrangement and the atmosphere. The shape, size, material or particular functional requirements of these mobile components determine their placement in the room and their relationship to the user.

Individual functional areas in a room are defined by, among other things, the arrangement and the shaping of space-defining elements. Along with vertical space delimiters such as walls and built-in units, horizontal enclosing elements such as ceilings and floors can be given a large role in defining individual functional zones. Even small height differences provide a view over the lower spatial zones and thus create borders between the respective areas, in other words they define new spatial areas. The interplay between higher and lower spatial zones differentiates between individual spatial areas and, additionally, contributes to changing spatial sequences.

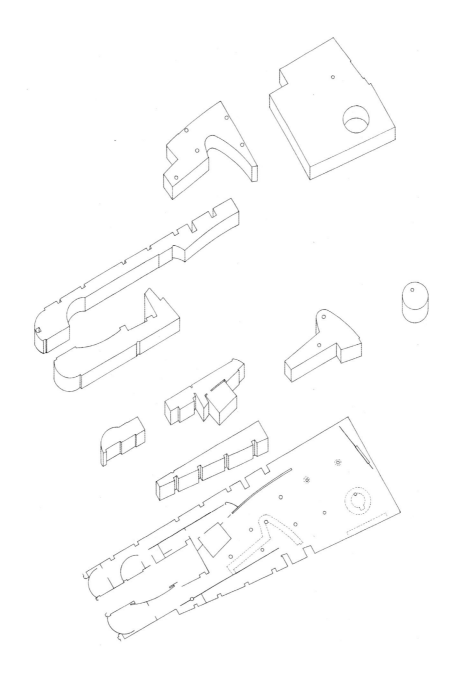

Raumkonzepte   *Spatial concepts*

Frank Lloyd Wright
Unity Temple, Chicago, 1907

»Ich glaube, das war wohl das erste Mal, dass der innere Raum als die eigentliche Realität des Gebäudes deutlich wurde. Wenn man im Tempel saß, saß man unter einer großen Betonplatte, die den Augen erlaubte, an vier Seiten bis in die Wolken zu blicken. Es gab auch keine Wände mit Löchern. Sie werden bemerken, dass der Betrachtende, das Gefühl der Annäherung bekommt, wo er auch sitzen mag. Und ich habe an dieser These schon lange gearbeitet, denn es ist mir klar geworden, dass, als ich das Gebäude baute, die Wirklichkeit des Gebäudes nicht in den Außenwänden und im Dach bestand, sondern in diesem inneren Raum, den man erlebte.«

Interview mit Frank Lloyd Wright. Frühjahr 1956.
(Caedmon Schallplatte TC 1064)

»Die großen Stützpfosten waren so in den Grundriss gesetzt, dass sie auf den vier Seiten des Raumes doppelte Nischen bildeten. Durchflutete man diese Seitennischen mit Licht von oben, erhielt man den Eindruck eines schönen, wolkenlosen Tages im Raum. Und mit diesem Gefühl für das Licht wurde die Mitteldecke zwischen den vier großen Pfosten zum Oberlicht; Tageslicht sickerte durch die Deckenfenster aus bernsteingelbem Glas zwischen den Betonbalken. So hatte das Licht die Wärme des Sonnenlichts.«

Wright, Frank Lloyd: *Ausgeführte Bauten und Entwürfe*.
Tübingen 1991.

"I think that was about the first time when the interior space began to come through as the reality of the building. When you sat in the Temple, you were sitting under a big concrete slab that let your eyes go out into the clouds on four sides. Then there were no walls with holes in them. You will notice that features were arranged against that interior space allowing a sense of it to come to the beholder wherever he happened to be. And I have been working on that thesis for a long time because it was dawning on me when I built that building that the reality of the building did not consist in the walls and in the roof, but in this space within to be lived in."

Interview with Frank Lloyd Wright. Spring 1956.
(Caedmon Record TC 1064)

"The large supporting posts were so set in plan as to form a double tier of alcoves on four sides of the room. I flooded these side-alcoves with light from above to get a sense of a happy cloudless day into the room. And with this feeling for light the center ceiling between the four great posts became skylight, daylight sifting through between the intersecting concrete beams, filtering through amber glass ceiling lights. Thus managed the light would, rain or shine, have the warmth of sunlight."

Wright, Frank Lloyd: *Ausgeführte Bauten und Entwürfe*.
Tübingen 1991.

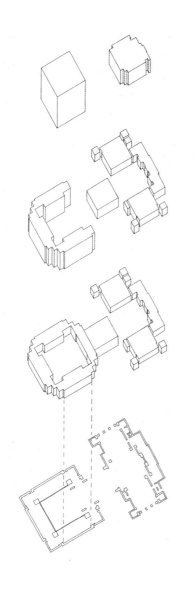

| Raumbildung | Spatial definition |
| Körper und Raum | Objects and space |

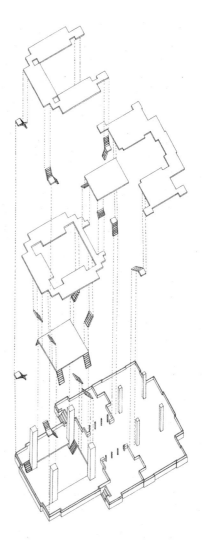

| Raumfolge | Spatial sequence |
| Orte und Wege | Places and paths |

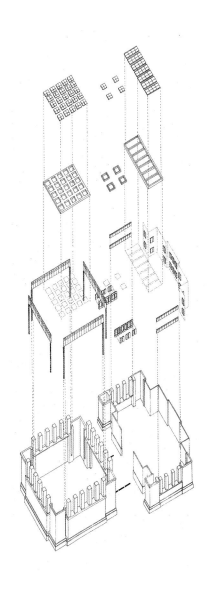

Raumgestalt
Material, Farbe, Licht

Spatial design
Material, color, light

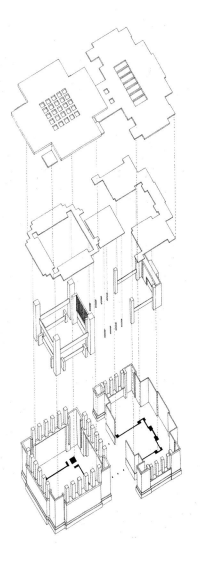

Raumstruktur
Form und Ordnung

Spatial structure
Form and order

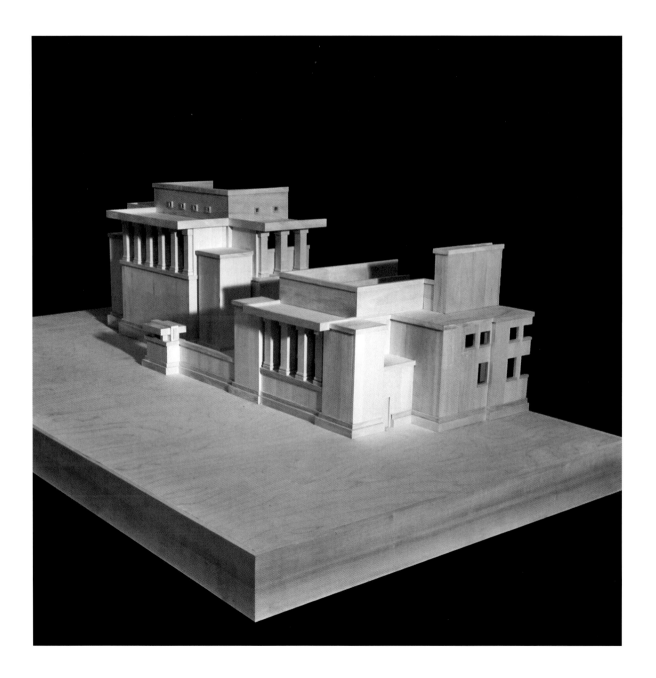

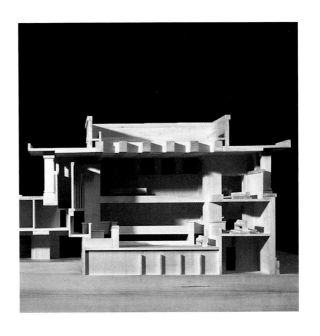

Frank Lloyd Wright
Haus für Frederick C. Robie, Frederick C. Robie House, Chicago, 1910

»Doch vorher schon war mir aus einem angeborenen Sinn für Behaglichkeit der Gedanke gekommen, dass die Größe der menschlichen Gestalt alle Maße einer Wohnung und die eines jeden Gegenstandes darin bestimmen müsste. Das menschliche Maß war das wahre Baumaß.

Ich erkannte, dass die Horizontale die Erdlinie des menschlichen Lebens war. Zunächst erweiterte ich den Raum in der Horizontalen, ohne das Gebäude zu vergrößern, indem ich auf Zwischenwände verzichtete. Ein ganz neues Gefühl für die Raumwerte in der Architektur entstand. Ich erhob die Plastizität zur Kontinuität in der Konzeption des Gebäudes als Ganzem.«

Wright, Frank Lloyd: *The natural house*. New York 1982.

"Before this, by way of innate sense of comfort, had come the idea that, in the matter of scale, the human being is the logical norm for a dwelling and every object in it. The human being is the true unit-of-size.

I recognized that the horizontal was the earth line of human life. First of all I extended space horizontally, without enlarging the building, by doing without partition walls. An entirely new sense of space-values in architecture resulted. I raised plasticity to continuity in the concept of the building as a whole. Let walls, ceilings, floors become not only party to each other but part of each other, reacting upon each other."

Wright, Frank Lloyd: *The Natural House*. New York 1982.

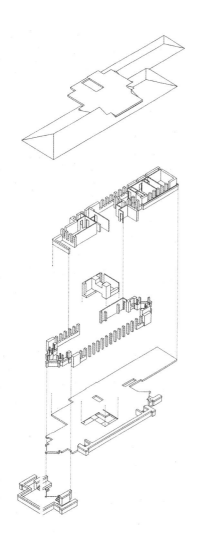
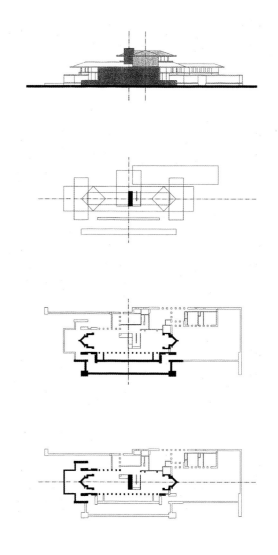

| Raumbildung | Spatial definition | Raumstruktur | Spatial structure |
| Körper und Raum | Objects and space | Form und Ordnung | Form and order |

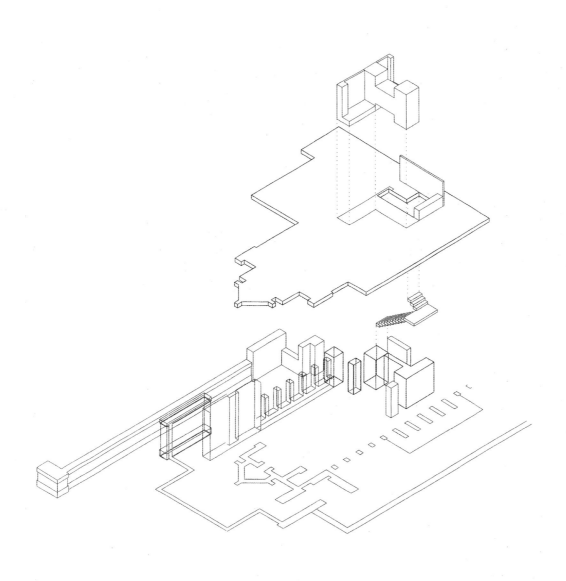

Raumfolge
Orte und Wege

Spatial sequence
Places and paths

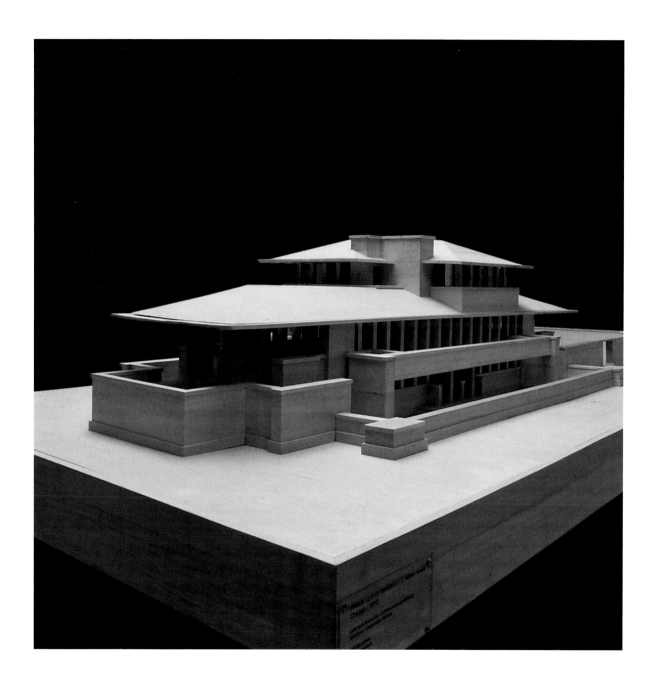

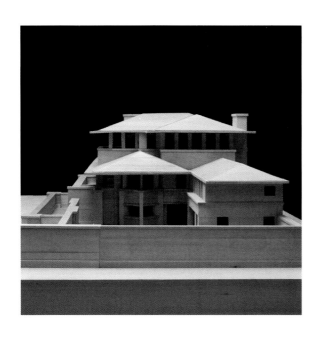 

Robert van 't Hoff
Villa Henny, Utrecht, 1919

»Der Entwurf eines Gebäudes entsteht aus der Komposition der Grundrisse. De facto sind die horizontalen Schnitte mit den in Zentimeter angegebenen Höhen schon der gesamte Entwurf in drei Dimensionen.«

»Um Stil in der Architektur zu erzielen, muss diese auch aus technischen Gesichtspunkten zur vollkommenen Perfektion gelangen und der Begriff ›Kunst‹ in den Hintergrund. Mit der Verwendung neuer Baustoffe wird eine logische Entwicklung der Form entstehen. Der Antagonismus zwischen neuer und alter Gestaltung wird durch Individualismus hervorgerufen.«

Van 't Hoff, Robert: *De Stijl*. März 1918.

"The design of a building develops out of the composition of its floor plan. The horizontal sections with their heights given to the centimeter are, de facto, the entire design in three dimensions."

"In order to achieve style, architecture must also reach technical perfection and any idea of 'art' must recede into the background. The use of new building materials will create a logical development of forms. The antagonism between the new plastic architecture and the old is a result of man's individualism."

Van 't Hoff, Robert: *De Stijl*. March 1918.

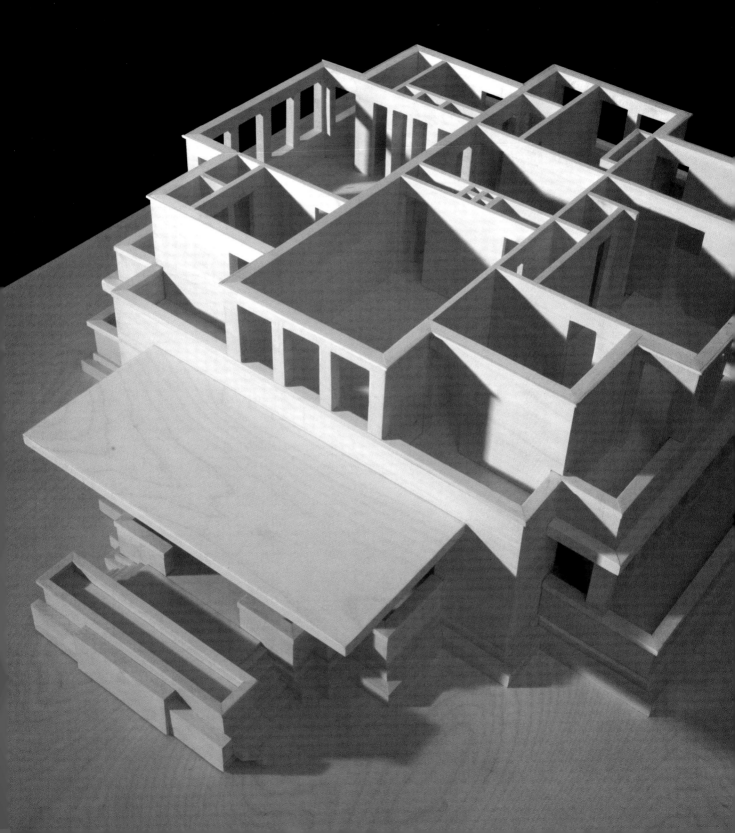

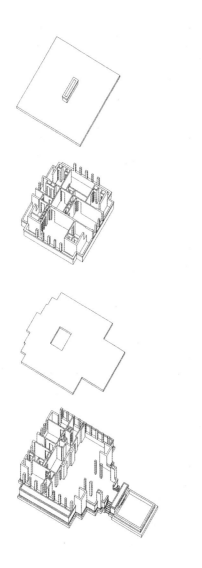

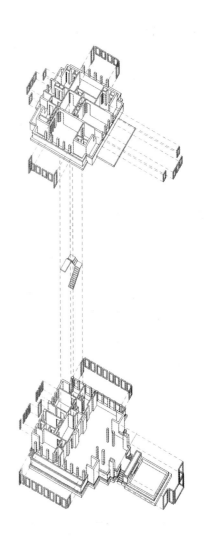

| Raumbildung | Spatial definition |
| Körper und Raum | Objects and space |

| Raumstruktur | Spatial structure |
| Form und Ordnung | Form and order |

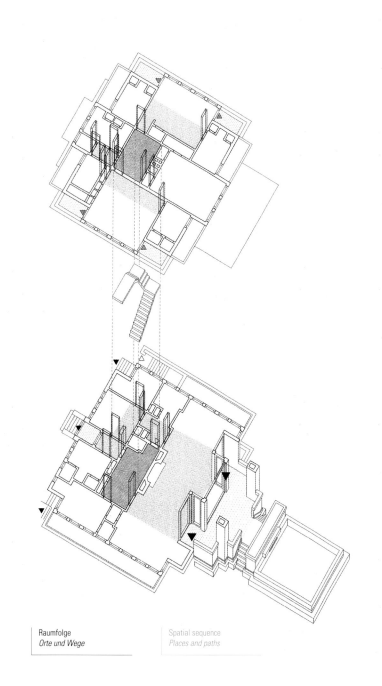

Raumfolge
Orte und Wege

Spatial sequence
Places and paths

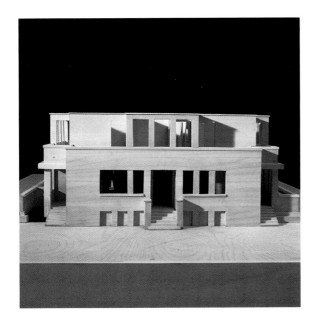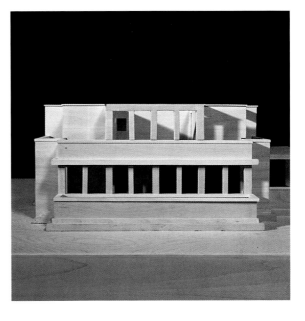

Theo van Doesburg, Cornelis van Eesteren
Maison Particulière, Paris, 1923

Aus dem 16-Punkte-Programm: *Auf dem Weg zu einer plastischen Architektur:*

»Die neue Architektur ist antikubisch, das heißt, sie versucht nicht, alle Funktions-Raumzellen in einen geschlossenen Würfel zusammenzufügen, sondern projiziert Funktions-Raumzellen (wie auch überhängende Flächen, Balkone usw.) zentrifugal vom Mittelpunkt des Würfels aus: so gewinnen Höhe, Breite und Tiefe plus Zeit einen ganz neuen plastischen Ausdruck in offenen Räumen. Auf diese Weise erreicht die Architektur einen mehr oder minder schwebenden Aspekt (soweit dies vom baulichen Standpunkt möglich ist – das ist ein Problem für den Ingenieur!), der sozusagen der Schwerkraft der Natur entgegenwirkt.«

»Die neue Architektur gestattet die Farbe organisch als direktes Mittel des Ausdrucks ihrer Beziehungen nicht real, sondern unsichtbar. Das Gleichgewicht organischer Beziehungen erhält nur durch das Mittel der Farbe sichtbare Realität.«

Van Doesburg, Theo. In: Conrads, Ulrich (Hg.): *Programme und Manifeste zur Architektur des 20. Jahrhunderts.* Berlin 1964.

From the 16-point program *Towards a plastic architecture:*

"The new architecture is anti-cubic; that is to say, it does not attempt to fit all the functional space cells together into a closed cube, but projects functional space-cells (as well as overhanging surfaces, balconies etc.) centrifugally from the centre of the cube outwards. Thus height, breadth and depth plus time gain an entirely new plastic expression. In this way architecture achieves a more or less floating aspect (in so far as this is possible from the constructional standpoint – this is a problem for the engineer!) which operates, as it were, in opposition to natural gravity."

"The new architecture permits color organically as a direct means of expressing its relationships within space and time. Without color these relationships are not real, but invisible. The balance of organic relationships acquires visible reality only by means of color."

Van Doesburg, Theo. In: Conrads, Ulrich (Ed.): *Programme und Manifeste zur Architektur des 20. Jahrhunderts.* Berlin 1964.

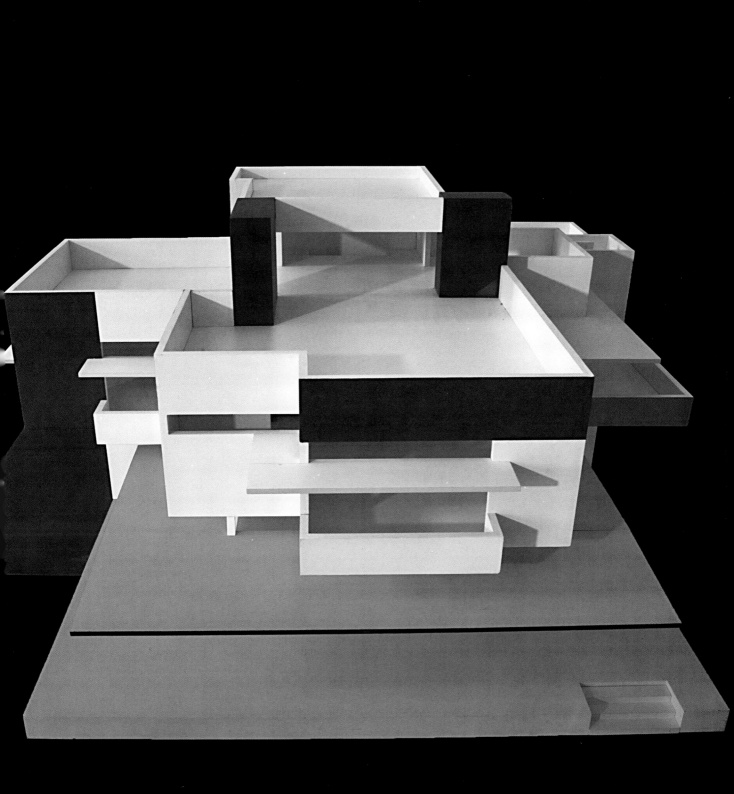

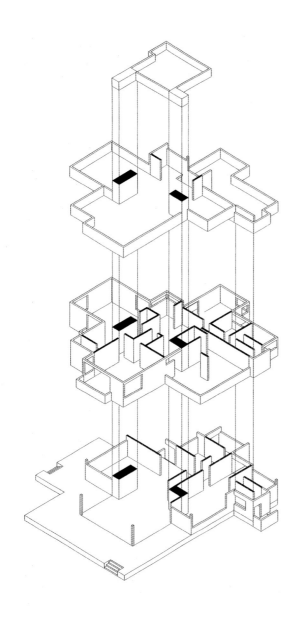

Raumbildung
Körper und Raum

Spatial definition
Objects and space

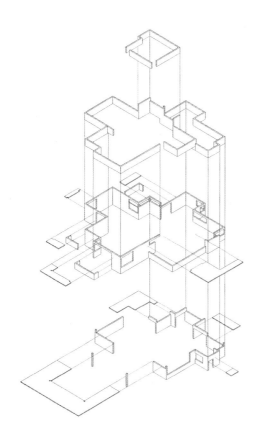

Raumstruktur
Äußere Struktur

Spatial structure
External structure

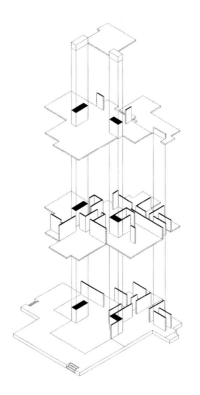

Raumstruktur
Innere Struktur

Spatial structure
Internal structure

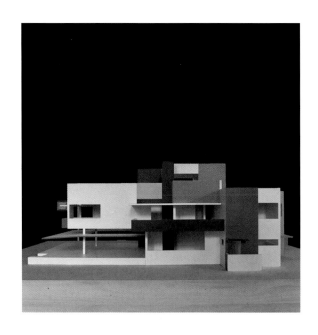

Gerrit T. Rietveld
Haus Schröder, Schroeder House, Utrecht, 1924

»Was Architektur auch immer bewirkt, niemals darf sie den Raum verschwenden. Architektur ist das, was unser räumliches Empfinden als Wirklichkeit erfasst. Das Material, die Gestalt und Farbe einer Stütze, einer Wand, eines Fensterrahmens oder eines Daches darf nicht im Vordergrund stehen. Wichtig ist der Inhalt des Werkes, das Umfeld und der Raum dazwischen. Wenn man dort gerne lebt, ist das auf die Qualität des Raumes zurückzuführen.«

Rietveld, Gerrit T.: *The Rietveld Schröder House*. Braunschweig 1988.

"Therefore I would like to make one thing clear: whatever architecture achieves, it should never waste space. Architecture is what makes our spatial experience reality. The material, form or color of a support, a wall, a window frame or a roof must not be in the foreground. What is important is the content of the structure, the surroundings and the space in between. If one enjoys living there, that is a result of the quality of the space."

Rietveld, Gerrit T.: *The Rietveld Schröder House*. Braunschweig 1988.

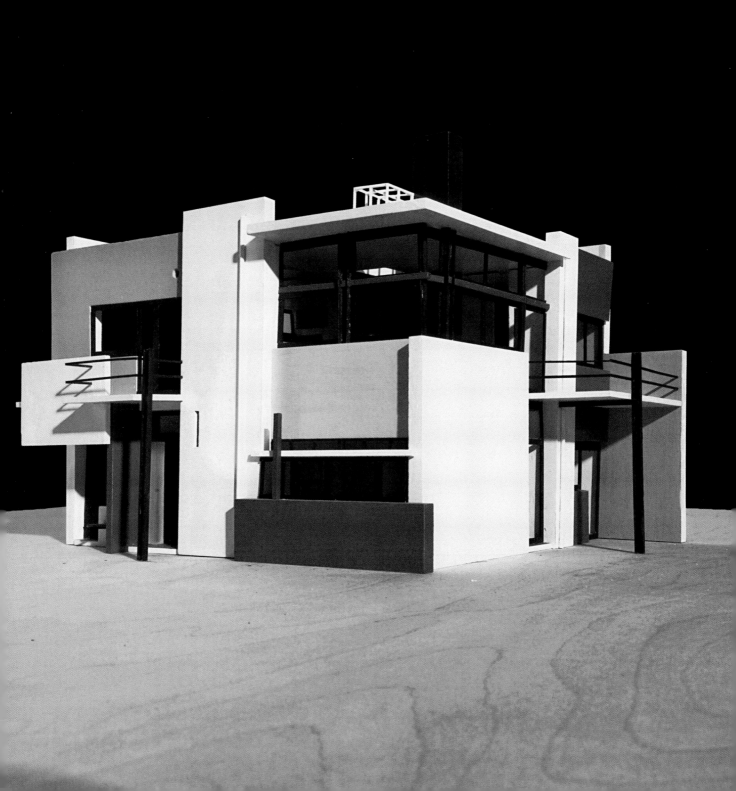

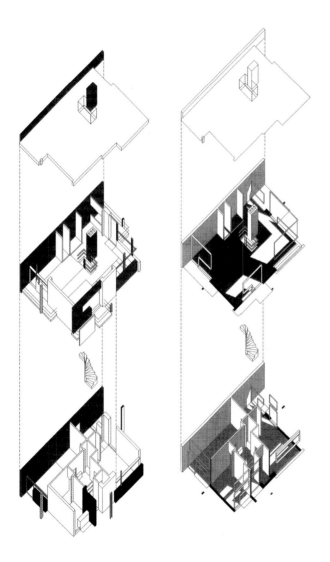

Raumgestalt
Material, Farbe, Licht

Spatial design
Material, color, light

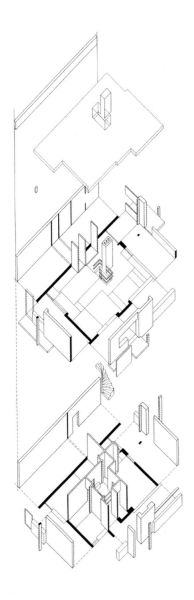

Raumstruktur
Form und Ordnung

Spatial structure
Form and order

Raumfunktion
Raum und Nutzung

Spatial function
Space and use

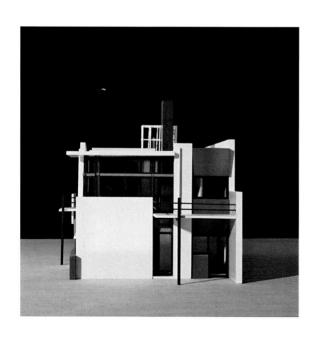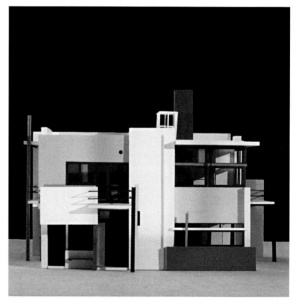

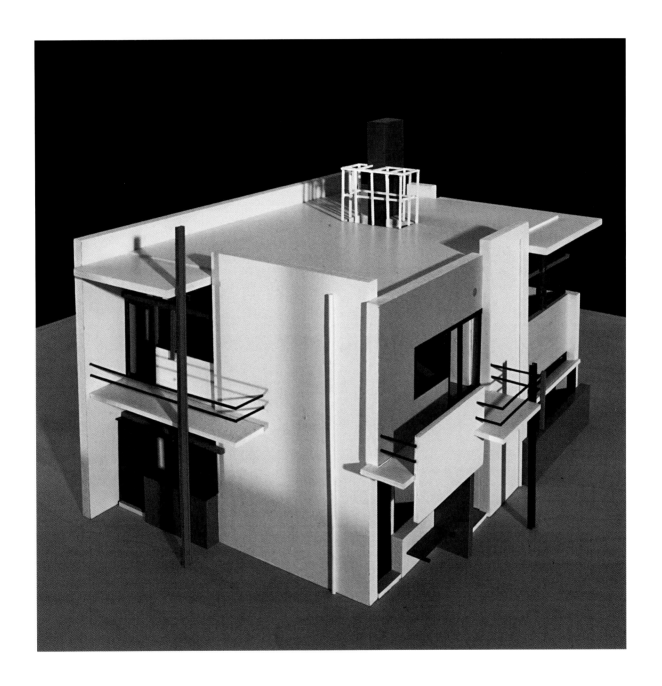

Le Corbusier
Pavillon de L'Esprit Nouveau, Paris, 1925

»Programm: das Kunstgewerbe verleugnen. Dafür aber bekräftigen, dass Architektur sich vom kleinsten Gebrauchsgegenstand im Hause bis auf die Straße, auf die Stadt, ja noch darüber hinaus erstreckt; zeigen, dass die Industrie durch ein Auswahlprinzip reine Gegenstände erzeugen kann, zeigen, dass eine Wohnung standardisiert werden kann, um den ›Serienmenschen‹ zu befriedigen. Die praktische, komfortable und schöne Wohnzelle, die wirkliche Wohnmaschine, häuft sich in Höhe und Ausdehnung zu einer großen Siedlung: zu immeublesvillas. Der Pavillon ist also eine solche Zelle des Wohnblocks, genauso konstruiert, wie wenn sich diese in 15 Metern Höhe über dem Boden befände: Wohnung und Etagengarten. In einem weiteren Raum, der Rotunde, befinden sich reiche Studien zum Städtebau: zwei Dioramen von 100 Quadratmetern; das eine die Dreimillionenstadt von 1922, das andere der ›Plan Voisin‹ von Paris. Ein neuer Begriff hat das Wort Mobiliar ersetzt. Das neue Wort wird Ausrüstung sein. Kästen ersetzen die unzähligen Möbelstücke verschiedenen Namens, Kästen, bald in der Wand, bald an die Wand gelehnt, und so verteilt, dass sie sich an jeder Stelle des Hauses befinden, wo eine bestimmte tägliche Arbeit stattfindet. Nur Tische und Stühle bleiben übrig.«

Le Corbusier: *Oeuvre complète. 1910–1925*. 1. Band. Zürich 1946.

"Program: to reject the decorative arts. To affirm that architecture extends from even the most humble furnishings in a home to the street, to the city, and even further. To show that industry, by virtue of a selective principle, can create pure forms, to show that a home can be standardized in order to satisfy the uniform needs of the human being. The practical, comfortable and aesthetically pleasing living unit, the true 'machine for living' is stacked and spread out to a large neighborhood of 'immeuble-villas' ('freehold maisonettes'). Thus the pavilion represents such a cell in an apartment block, constructed as though it was to be found at a height of 15 meters over the ground: apartment and hanging garden. A number of urban planning studies can be found in an additional room, the rotunda: two 100 square meters dioramas; one of the City of 3 Million from the year 1922 and the other the 'Plan Voisin' of Paris. A new word has replaced 'furniture'. That new word is 'equipment'. Storage units (casiers) replace innumerable pieces of furniture of various names; casiers in a wall, leaning against a wall, placed at every point in the home where a particular daily activity is performed. Only chairs and tables remain."

Le Corbusier: *Oeuvre complète. 1910–1925*. Vol. 1. Zurich 1946.

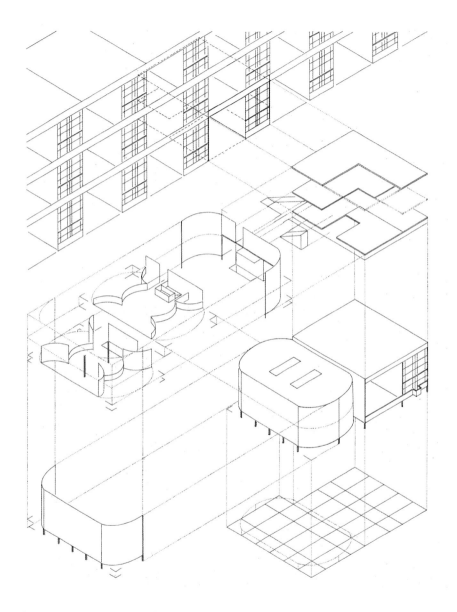

Raumbildung
Körper und Raum

Spatial definition
Objects and space

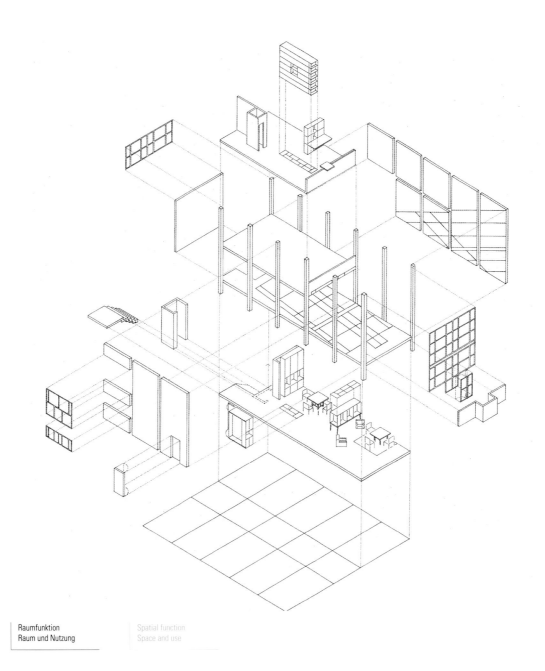

Raumfunktion
Raum und Nutzung

Spatial function
Space and use

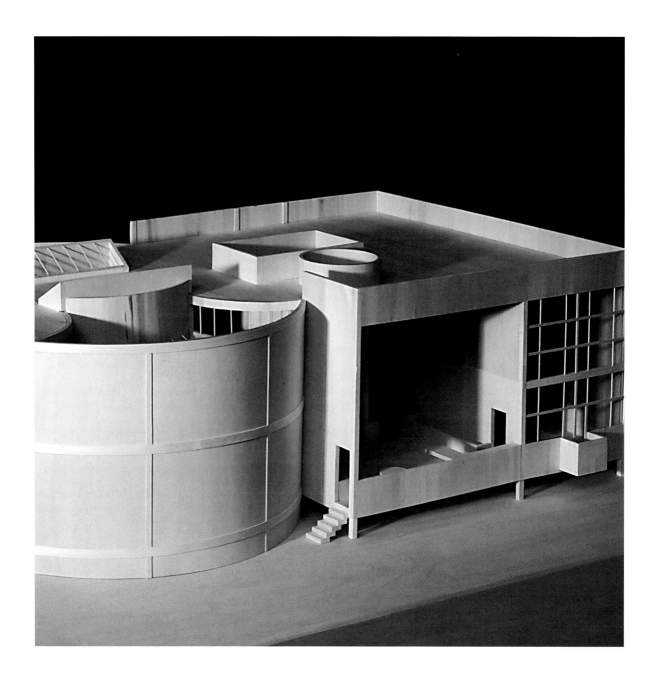

Walter Gropius
Meisterhaus Feininger, Dessau, 1926

»Vereinfachung durch Multiplizierung bedeutet Verbilligung und Beschleunigung. Der Grundriss der einen der beiden Wohnungen ist das verschränkte, um 90 Grad von Ost nach Süd gedrehte Spiegelbild des Grundrisses der anderen. Genau die gleichen Bauteile sind verwendet, die Ansicht beider Hälften aber durch die Verschränkung verschieden. Die von der Wandmalereiabteilung des Bauhauses durchgeführte farbige Gestaltung betont die räumliche Organisation innerhalb der Wohnung, bringt aber gleichzeitig starke Variation in die Wirkung an sich gleicher Räume. Das Raumgefühl verändert sich; während die alten Zeiten abgeschlossener Kulturentwicklungen die schwere Erdgebundenheit in festen monolit wirkenden Baukörpern und individualisierten Innenräumen verkörpern, zeigen die Werke der heutigen richtunggebenden Baumeister ein verändertes Raumempfinden, das die Bewegung, den Verkehr, unserer Zeit in einer Auflockerung des Innenraumes mit dem Allraum zu erhalten sucht, was die abschließende Wand verneint.«

»Ebenso wünschen wir uns auch unser erweitertes Kleid, die Wohnung, befreit von sinnlosem, raumsperrenden Kram und überflüssigen Verzierungen. Der Willkür der Stile sind wir satt geworden, von der Laune zur Regel geschritten und suchen nun in klaren, knappen und einfachen Formen, die der Art unseres heutigen Lebens entsprechen, den wesentlichen und sinnfälligen Ausdruck unserer häuslichen Umgebung.«

Gropius, Walter: *Bauhausbauten Dessau*. 1930.

"All six semi-detached homes are the same down to the last detail and yet they differ in their impact. Simplification through multiplication means economization and acceleration. The floor plan of one of the two units is the mirror image, offset 90 degree from east to south, of that of the other unit. Though the same structural elements are employed, the view of each half presents itself differently due to the rotation. The color scheme used by the Bauhaus wall painting department stresses the spatial organization within the homes while greatly varying the effect of rooms which are, essentially, the same. Our sense of space is changing; whereas former periods of cultural development emphasized their earthbound nature through static, monolithic structures and individualized interiors, the works of the trend-setters among current architects show a changed perception of space which attempts to preserve the movement, the traffic flow, of our time in a more relaxed relationship between interiors and space as a whole, saying no to enclosing walls."

"In the same way, we would like our extended clothing, our living space, to be free of meaningless, cumbersome junk and of superfluous decoration. We've become tired of arbitrariness of styles, gone from a whim to a rule, and we now seek, in clear, concise and simple forms consistent with our present way of life, the central and manifest expression of our home environment."

Gropius, Walter: *Bauhausbauten Dessau*. 1930.

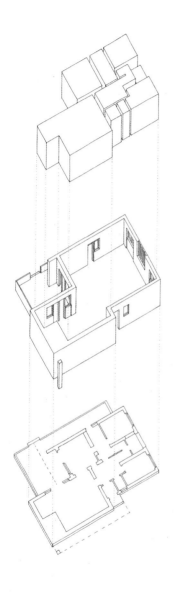
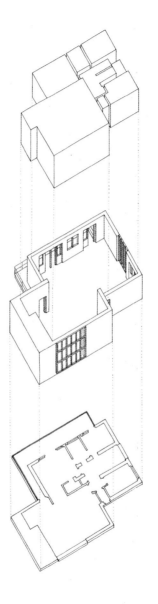

Raumbildung
Körper und Raum

Spatial definition
Objects and space

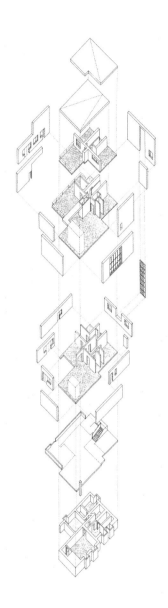
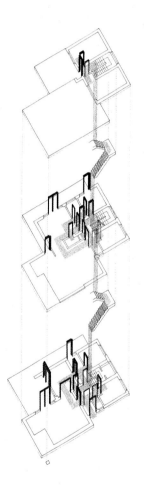

| Raumstruktur | Spatial structure | Raumfolge | Spatial sequence |
| Form und Ordnung | Form and order | Orte und Wege | Places and paths |

Hans Scharoun
Haus 33, House 33, Weißenhofsiedlung, Stuttgart, 1927

»Das Haus 33 ist aus Freude am Spiel mit neuem Material und neuen Forderungen an den Raum geworden. Das Organisatorische eines Wirtschaftsflügels, das kabinenhafte des Schlafnutzraumes, die Verbundenheit von Innen- und Außenraum, die Möglichkeit des Einanderzuwendens und Voneinanderabwendens im Wohnraum, sind Ausgangspunkte für die Gestaltung gewesen. Allzu viel Typisiertes findet der Betrachter nicht. Das ›Vielfältige‹ im ›Eigenheim‹ wird Norm erst bei serienmäßiger Herstellung.«

Scharoun, Hans: *Bau und Wohnung*. Stuttgart 1927.

»Zum Hause selbst: Es sollte in seinen Dispositionen klar sein. Absolut und relativ maßstäblich groß wirken. Dies suchte ich zu erreichen: durch klare Scheidung von Wohn-, Schlaf- und Wirtschaftsabteilung, durch starke Maßunterschiede der Wohn- und Schlafräume, durch die Vereinigung verschiedener Wohnfunktionen in einer Raumeinheit, durch das Spiel der durch das ganze Haus führenden Achse als Linie gegen Raum (Ausklang dieser Achse im Garten sollte ein längliches Wasserbecken sein, das aus wirtschaftlichen Gründen nicht zur Ausführung kam), durch die Form des Wohnraums, die Weite über das mauerwerksmäßig Begrenzte fühlen lässt, durch weitgehende Einbeziehung der – hier besonders schönen – Landschaft.«

Scharoun, Hans: Brief an W. Lotz. In: *Die Form*. Berlin 1927.

"House Number 33 developed out of the pleasure of playing with new material and new demands on space. The organizational aspects of the utility wing, the cabin-like nature of the bedroom, the interconnection between interior and exterior space, the possibility of turning towards or from one another in the living-room, these were all starting points for the design. The viewer will not find much standardization. 'Manifoldness' in 'private' homes becomes the norm only when these are constructed in series."

Scharoun, Hans: *Bau und Wohnung*. Stuttgart 1927.

"Regarding the house itself: Its disposition should be clear. To appear spacious in both absolute and relative terms. I attempted to achieve this: through clear separation of living, sleeping and working space, through definite dimensional differences between living and sleeping quarters, through the combination of various living functions in one room unit, through the effect of the axis extending through the entire house as a line against a space (the conclusion of the axis in the garden was to be an elongate pond, which for financial reasons was left unbuilt), through the shape of the living-room, which offers a feeling of space beyond the limits of its walls, through extensive inclusion of the – in this case particularly beautiful – landscape."

Scharoun, Hans: Letter to W. Lotz. In: *Die Form*. Berlin 1927.

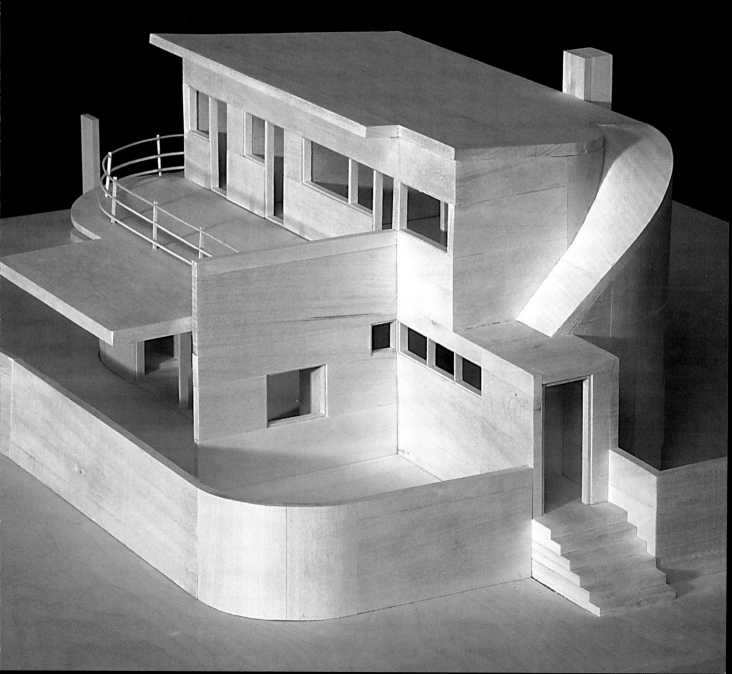

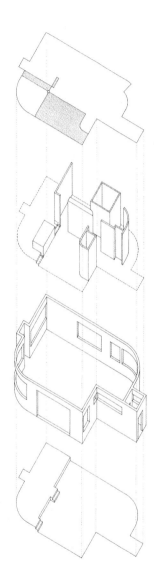
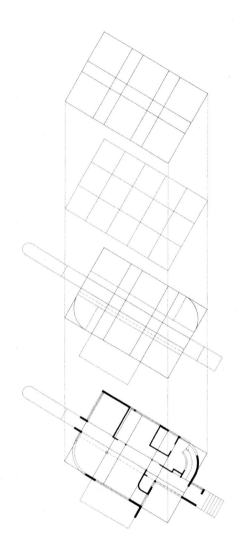

Raumbildung
Körper und Raum

Spatial definition
Objects and space

Raumstruktur
Form und Ordnung

Spatial structure
Form and order

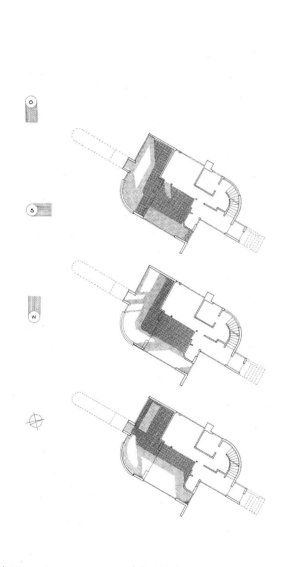
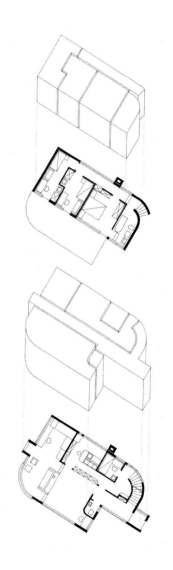

| Raumgestalt | Spatial design | Raumfunktion | Spatial function |
| Material, Farbe, Licht | Material, color, light | Raum und Nutzung | Space and use |

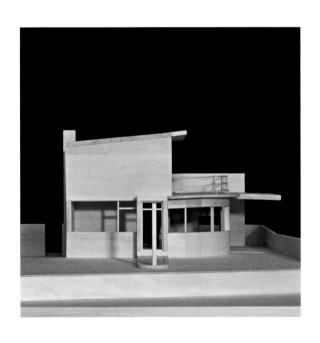 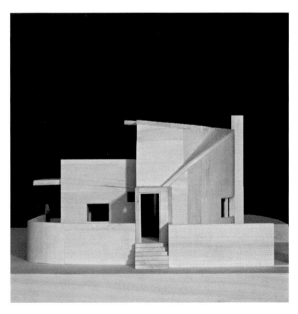

Theo van Doesburg
Café de l'Aubette, Straßburg, Strasbourg, 1928

»Die Grundrisse trugen gewiss die Merkmale einer großstädtischen Betriebsamkeit. Die wichtigsten Materialien, die für die Ausführung der Innenräume nach den modernsten Erfordernissen verwendet wurden, sind: Beton, Eisen, Spiegelglas, Aluminium, Nickel, Hartkautschuk, Terrazzo, Linoleum, Gummi, Parkett, Fliesen, Duralumin usw. Es wurde von einer gleichmäßig hellen und doch sanften Beleuchtung ausgegangen, um Schatten soweit wie möglich zu verhindern. Das große ›Cine-Dancing‹ wird indirekt beleuchtet, durch Reflektoren an Nickelstangen, die sich über die gesamte Länge des Saales hinziehen. Da sowohl die Fenster als auch die Türen und alle anderen die Wand durchbrechenden Elemente einen stark orthogonalen Akzent hatten, war dieser Saal besonders dafür geeignet, eine schräge, eigenständige Farbeinteilung, die in der Lage war, der Spannung der Architektur zu widerstehen, aufzunehmen. Die Kompositionen an den Decken und Wänden sind aus zwei Gründen reliefartig ausgeführt. Erstens um eine strenge Abgeschlossenheit der Flächen zu erreichen und Farbinterferenzen zu verhindern, und zweitens um ein zufälliges oder willkürliches Zusammenfließen der Flächen zu vermeiden. Licht und Farbe waren in diesem Festsaal gleichermaßen von funktionaler Bedeutung.«

Van Doesburg, Theo: *Über europäische Architektur, gesammelte Aufsätze*. In: *Het Bouwbedrijf 1924–1931*. Berlin 1990.

"The floor plan was clearly characteristic of metropolitan hustle and bustle. The most important materials that were used for the interior according to the most modern prerequisites are: concrete, iron, plate glass, aluminum, nickel, ebonite, terrazzo, linoleum, rubber, parquet, tiles, duralumin etc. The lighting was to be evenly bright and yet soft, in order to avoid shadows as much as possible. The large 'Ciné-Dancing' is indirectly lighted by reflectors on nickel rods that extend along the entire length of the hall. As both the windows and the doors and all the other elements that interrupt the walls had a strong orthogonal accent, this hall was particularly suited to diagonal, independent color elements that were capable of withstanding the tension of the architecture. There were two reasons for doing the designs on the ceilings and walls in relief: first of all, to achieve strict limits to the individual shapes and thus prevent color interferences, and secondly, to avoid random or arbitrary merging of the shapes. Light and color were of equal functional significance in this ballroom, and given that tables and chairs were only set up for banquets, the permanent furnishings truly consisted of only color and light."

Van Doesburg, Theo: *Über europäische Architektur, gesammelte Aufsätze*. In: *Het Bouwbedrijf 1924–1931*. Berlin 1990.

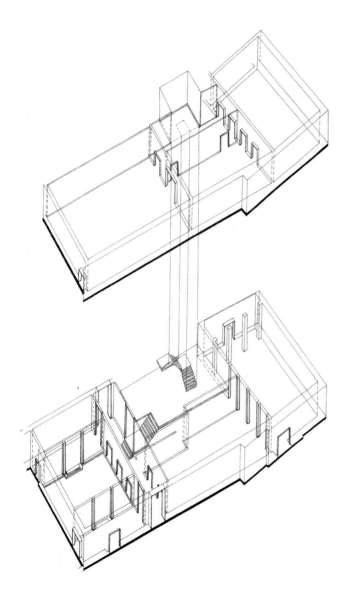

Raumfolge
Orte und Wege

Spatial sequence
Places and paths

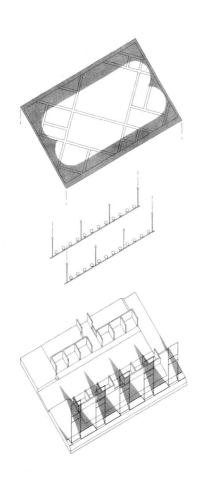
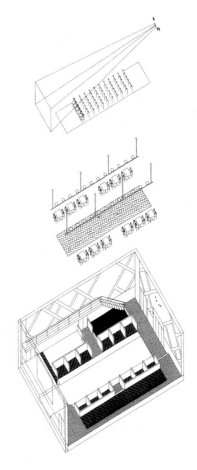

Raumgestalt
Material, Farbe, Licht

Spatial design
Material, color, light

Raumfunktion
Raum und Nutzung

Spatial function
Space and use

Ludwig Mies van der Rohe
Barcelona-Pavillon, 1929

»Die gläserne Haut, die gläsernen Wände erst lassen dem Skelettbau seine eindeutige konstruktive Gestalt und sichern ihm seine architektonischen Möglichkeiten. Nicht nur in den großen Zweckbauten. Es sind echte Bauelemente und Träger einer neuen Baukunst. Sie lassen ein Maß an Freiheit in der räumlichen Gestaltung, auf die wir nicht mehr verzichten werden. Jetzt erst können wir den Raum frei gliedern, ihn öffnen und in die Landschaft binden. Jetzt zeigt sich wieder, was Wand und Öffnung ist, was Boden und Decke. Die Einfachheit der Konstruktion, die Klarheit der tektonischen Mittel und die Reinheit des Materials tragen den Glanz ursprünglicher Schönheit.«

Mies van der Rohe, Ludwig: *Das kunstlose Wort* (Prospekt des Vereins Deutscher Spiegelglas-Fabrikanten). Berlin 1986.

»Die neue Zeit ist eine Tatsache; sie existiert unabhängig davon, ob wir ja oder nein zu ihr sagen. Sie ist weder besser noch schlechter als irgendeine andere Zeit. Nicht auf das was, sondern einzig und allein auf das wie kommt es an.«

Mies van der Rohe, Ludwig: *Die Form*. Ebenda.

"The glass skin and indeed the glass walls are needed to allow the frame construction its unequivocal constructive form and secure its architectural possibilities. Not only in large functional buildings. These are the construction elements and supports of a new architecture. They provide a degree of freedom in spatial design which we will come to expect. Only now can we organize space freely, opening it and linking it to the landscape. Now wall and opening, ceiling and floor show themselves. The simplicity of the construction, the clarity of the tectonic means and the purity of the material carry the splendor of original beauty."

Mies van der Rohe, Ludwig: *Das kunstlose Wort* (Brochure of the Verein Deutscher Spiegelglas-Fabrikanten). Berlin 1986.

"The new age is a fact; it exists regardless of whether we say 'yes' or 'no' to it. But it is neither better nor worse than any other age. It's not a question of what but solely of how."

Mies van der Rohe, Ludwig: *Die Form*. Ibid.

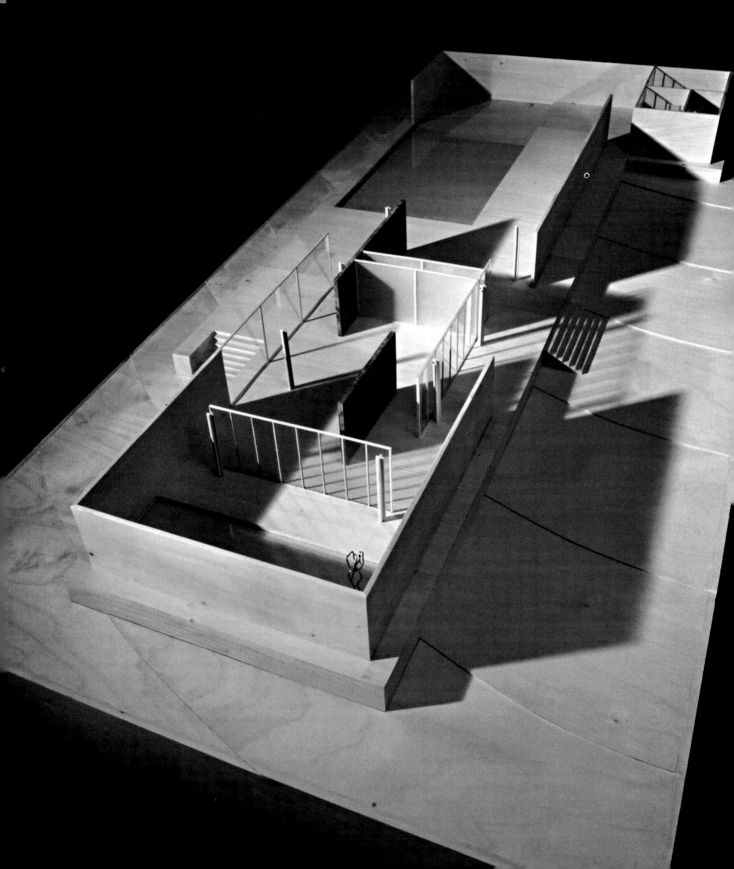

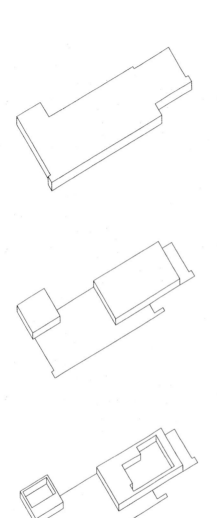
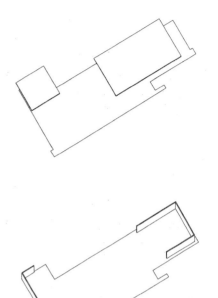
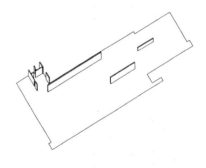

| Raumbildung | Spatial definition | Raumstruktur | Spatial structure |
| *Körper und Raum* | *Objects and space* | *Form und Ordnung* | *Form and order* |

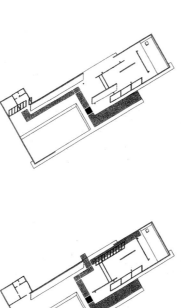
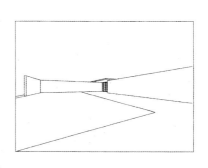
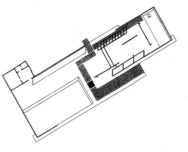
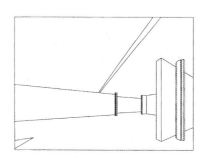
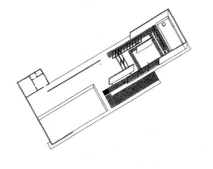
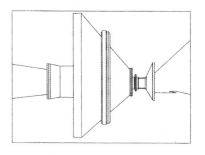

Raumfolge
Orte und Wege

Spatial sequence
Places and paths

Le Corbusier
Villa Savoye, Poissy, 1931

»Die Besucher drehen sich im Inneren des Gebäudes um und um und fragen sich, was das alles soll; sie können die Gründe all dessen, was sie sehen und empfinden, kaum begreifen; sie finden hier nichts mehr von dem, was man sonst ein ›Haus‹ nennt. Das Haus ist eine in der Luft hängende ›Schachtel‹, über die gesamte Länge zieht sich ohne Unterbrechung ein Fensterband. Um das Haus herum – zwischen den Stützpfeilern hindurch – läuft ein Fahrweg. Die Biegung umschließt, unter den Pfeilern, den Hauseingang, das Vestibül, die Garage. Die Autos kommen an und fahren ab oder parken – alles unter dem Haus. Vom Innern des Vestibüls aus führt eine Rampe, deren Ansteigen durch den geringen Neigungswinkel kaum wahrnehmbar ist, zur ersten Etage, in der sich das Leben der Bewohner abspielt. Die verschiedenen Zimmer, die Beleuchtung und Aussicht durch das um das Haus herumlaufende Fenster erhalten, führen strahlenförmig zu einem Hängegarten, der gleichsam ein Verteiler von Licht und Sonne ist. Vom Hängegarten aus geht die Rampe – jetzt im Freien – auf das Dach, auf die Sonnenterrasse. Von der Sonnenterrasse aus führt eine Wendeltreppe direkt in den Keller. Diese Wendeltreppe, ein rein vertikales Element, ›fügt sich‹ frei in die horizontale Komposition ein.«

Le Corbusier: *Feststellungen* (Vortrag in Buenos Aires 1929). Braunschweig 1987.

"Visitors turn round and round inside the building and ask themselves what is going on; they can hardly grasp the reasons behind what they see and feel; they find none of what is usually referred to as a 'house'. The house is a 'box in the air', uninterrupted ribbon windows extend across the entire length. A driveway leads around the house – between the pilotis – in the form of a hairpin. The turn encloses, directly under the columns, the entrance, the vestibule, the garage. The cars come and go or park – all under the house. A ramp with an almost imperceptible inclination leads from inside the vestibule to the first floor, the center of daily life for the inhabitants. The various rooms, which obtain their light and their view through the windows that run around the house, radiate out toward a hanging garden which spreads both light and sun. The ramp – now on the outside – rises from the hanging garden up to the roof, to the sun terrace. From the sun terrace, a spiral staircase leads directly to the basement. This spiral staircase, a purely vertical element, 'defers' freely to the horizontal composition. The plan is clear; it is tailored exactly to the requirements. And it blends well into the rural surroundings of Poissy."

Le Corbusier: *Feststellungen* (Lecture in Buenos Aires 1929). Braunschweig 1987.

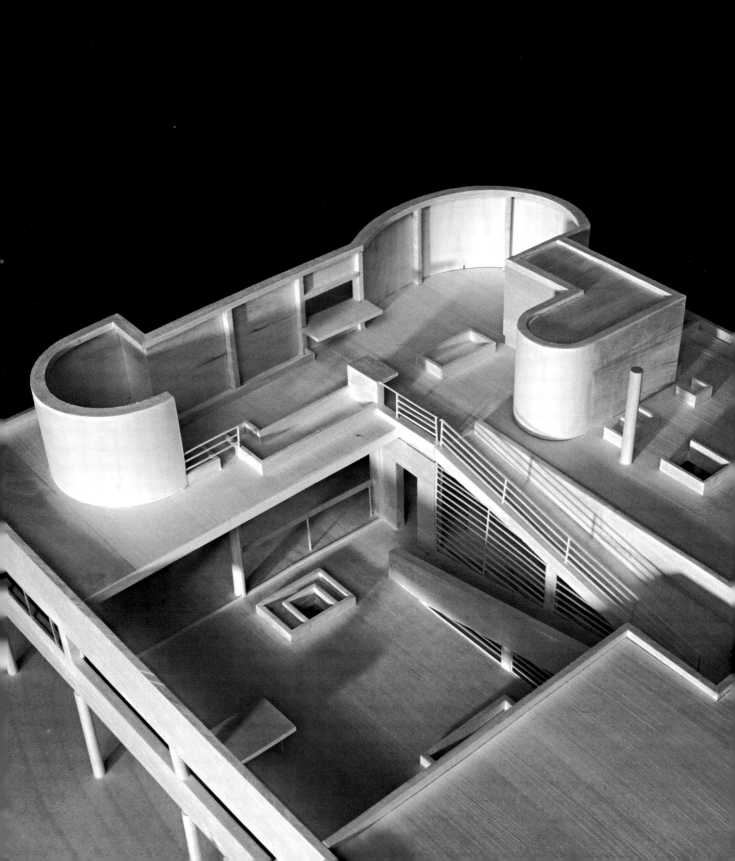

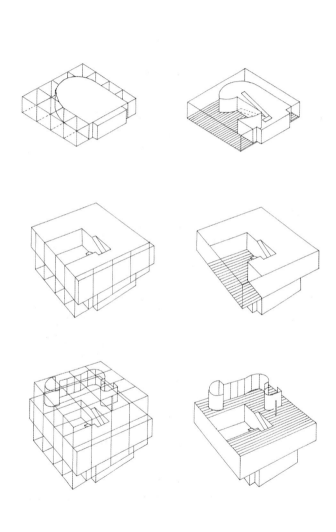
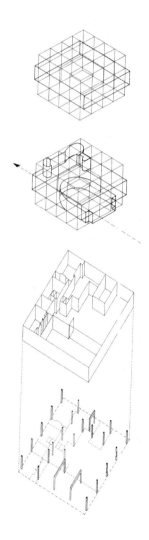

| Raumbildung | Spatial definition | Raumstruktur | Spatial structure |
| Körper und Raum | Objects and space | Form und Ordnung | Form and order |

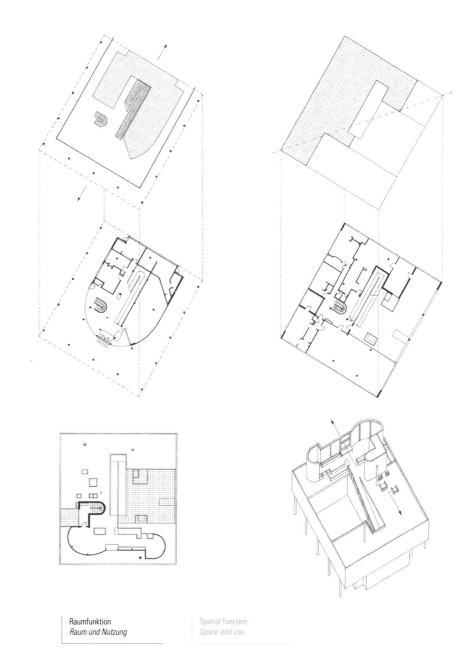

Raumfunktion
Raum und Nutzung

Spatial function
Space and use

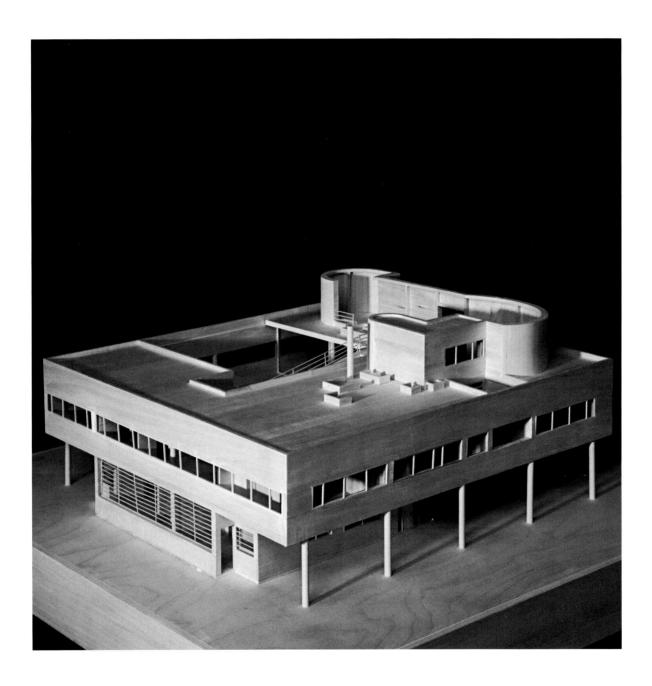

Frank Lloyd Wright
Haus E. J. Kaufmann, E. J. Kaufmann House, Fallingwater, Mill Run, 1939

»Ich entwickelte eine Liebe zu dir, weit über die gewöhnliche Beziehung zwischen Bauherrn und Architekten hinaus. Diese Liebe schenkte dir Fallingwater. Du wirst in deinem Leben nie wieder sowas haben.«

Wright, Frank Lloyd: *Fallingwater Rising*. New York 2004.

»Fallingwater ist ein großer Segen – einer der großen Segen, die man auf dieser Erde erfahren kann. Ich glaube, es glich bisher nichts dieser Koordination, dem mitfühlenden Ausdruck des großen Prinzips der Ruhe, wo Wald und Bach und Stein und die ganzen Elemente der Struktur so leise miteinander verbunden sind, dass man wirklich keinerlei Geräusche lauscht, obwohl die Musik des Bachs da ist. Aber Fallingwater hört man, wie man sich die ländliche Stille anhört.«

Wright, Frank Lloyd: *Fallingwater Rising*. New York 2004.

»Das Haus soll zu einer Serie von kleinen, anspruchsvollen Pavillons werden, die untereinander durch Galerien und Gänge verbunden sind.«

Wright, Frank Lloyd. In: Treiber, Daniel: *Frank Lloyd Wright*. Basel 1988.

»Die Aufmerksamkeit wird durch niedrige Decken nach außen gelenkt. Kein Fürstensaal bestimmt das Bild, sondern die lichten Strukturen der in rhythmischer Folge eingerahmten Waldlandschaft. Die Materialien des Bauwerks stimmen mit der Färbung der Felsen und Bäume überein. Für gelegentliche Farbtupfer sorgen helle Möbel, wie die Wildblumen oder Vögel draußen.«

Wright, Frank Lloyd. In: Curtis, William J. R.: *Architektur im 20. Jahrhundert*. Stuttgart 1989.

"I conceived a love of you quite beyond the ordinary relationship of client and Architect. That love gave you Fallingwater. You will never have anything more in your life like it."

Wright, Frank Lloyd: *Fallingwater Rising*. New York 2004.

"Fallingwater is a great blessing – one of the great blessings to be experienced here on earth. I think nothing yet ever equaled the coordination, sympathetic expression of the great principle of repose where forest and stream and rock and all the elements of structure are combined so quietly that really you listen not to any noise whatsoever although the music of the stream is there. But you listen to Fallingwater the way you listen to the quiet of the country."

Wright, Frank Lloyd: *Fallingwater Rising*. New York 2004.

"The house could become a series of delicate small pavilions, linked to each other by means of galleries or promenades."

Wright, Frank Lloyd. In: Treiber, Daniel: *Frank Lloyd Wright*. Basel 1988.

"Their attention is directed to the outside through low ceilings. No lordly hall sets the scene, instead the luminous features of the woodlands rhythmically enframed. The materials of the structure blend in with the colorings of the rocks and trees. Occasional dabs of color are provided by the bright furnishings, like the wildflowers and birds outside."

Wright, Frank Lloyd. In: Curtis, William J. R.: *Architektur im 20. Jahrhundert*. Stuttgart 1989.

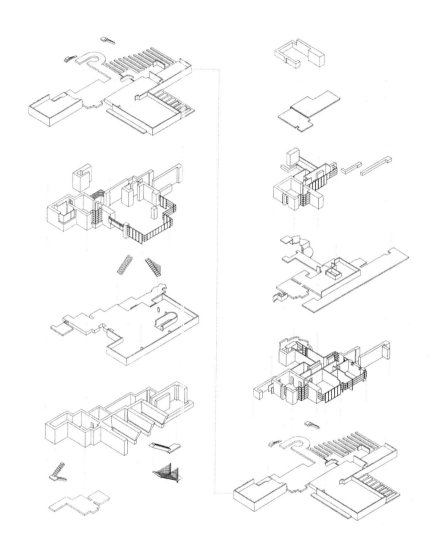

Raumbildung
Körper und Raum

Spatial definition
Objects and space

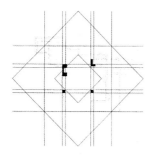

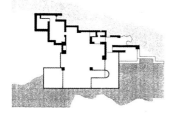

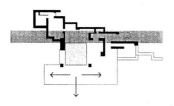

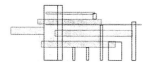

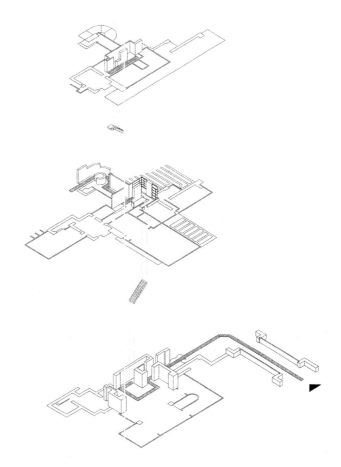

Raumstruktur	Spatial structure		Raumfolge	Spatial sequence
Form und Ordnung	*Form and order*		*Orte und Wege*	*Places and paths*

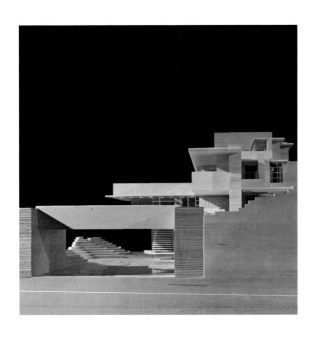 

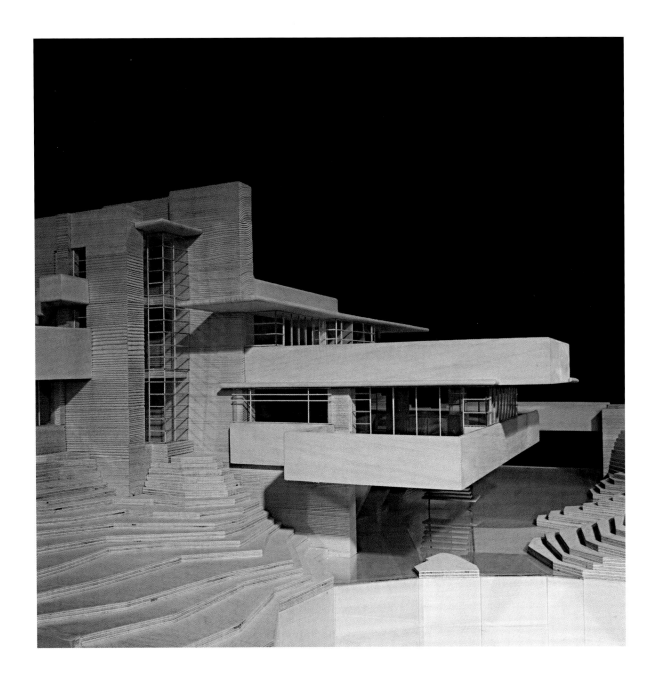

Charles & Ray Eames
Eames House, Pacific Palisades, Los Angeles, 1949

»Die meisten Baustoffe und Verfahren, die hier zum Einsatz kamen, sind Standards in der Bauindustrie, aber in vielen Fällen nicht üblich für Wohnbauten. Es war nicht schwierig, innerhalb der Struktur, die sich aus den Materialien und Techniken ergab, angenehme Wohn- und Arbeitsräume unterzubringen. Die tatsächliche Einteilung ist innerhalb der Gesamtstruktur jedoch sehr individuell. Interessant für das Versuchshausprogramm ist die Frage, inwieweit die Rigidität des Entwurfs verantwortlich ist für eine freie Raumnutzung. Interessant ist auch zu sehen, wie die sachlichste Gliederung doch zu Mustern und Strukturierungen führte. Die Farbe wurde als strukturelles Element eingesetzt; ihre Verwendung auf den verschiedenen Ebenen der Konstruktion wurde sorgfältig überlegt, das dunkle, warme Grau, das die tragenden Stahlteile und die metallenen Schiebefensterrahmen deckt, ist jedoch am erfreulichsten. Die konstante Kraft dieser Linien drückt deutlicher als alles andere aus, was in der strukturellen Hülle des Gebäudes vor sich geht. Dieses graue Gerüst umfasst in großer Geschlossenheit die verputzten Wandflächen in weiß, blau, rot, schwarz und erdfarben.

Ich habe den Wunsch, ein Zuhause zu haben, das nicht, wie allzu viele Häuser, wie ein dickes, dummes Kind herumsitzt und darauf wartet, bedient zu werden. Das Haus darf für sich selbst keine zwingenden Forderungen stellen.«

Eames, Charles: *Eames House*. Berlin 1994.

"Most materials and techniques which have been used here are standard to the building industry, but in many cases not standard to residential architecture. In the structural system that evolved from these materials and technologies, it was not difficult to create a pleasant space for living and working. The actual arrangement within the structure as a whole is, however, very individual. Case Study-wise it was interesting to consider how the rigidity of the system was responsible for the free use of space and to see how the most matter-of-fact structure resulted in pattern and texture. Color was planned and used as a structural element, and while much concern was given to its use in the various structural planes, the most gratifying of all the painted surfaces is the dark warm gray that covers the structural steel and the metal sash. The varying thickness and constant strength of this line does more than anything else to express what goes on in the structural web that surrounds the building. It is also this gray web that holds in a unit the stucco panels of white, blue, red, black and earth.

I want to have a home that does not, like all too many homes, sit about like a fat idiot child and demand to be waited on. The house must make no insistent demands of itself."

Eames, Charles: *Eames House*. Berlin 1994.

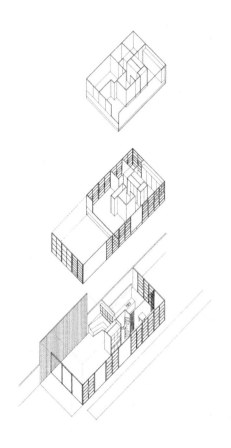
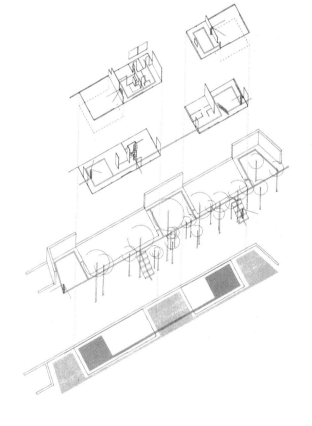

| Raumbildung | Spatial definition |
| Körper und Raum | Objects and space |

| Raumfolge | Spatial sequence |
| Orte und Wege | Places and paths |

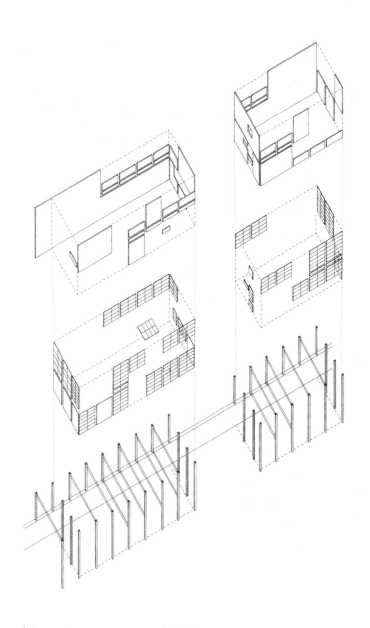

Raumgestalt
Material, Farbe, Licht

Spatial design
Material, color, light

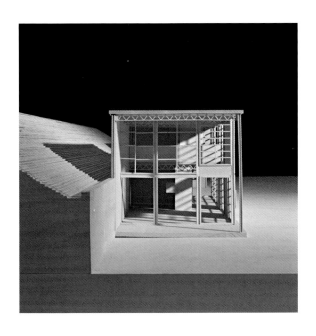

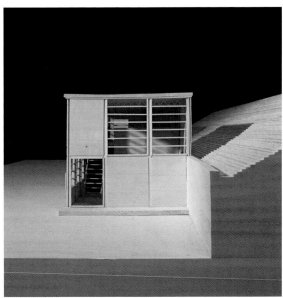

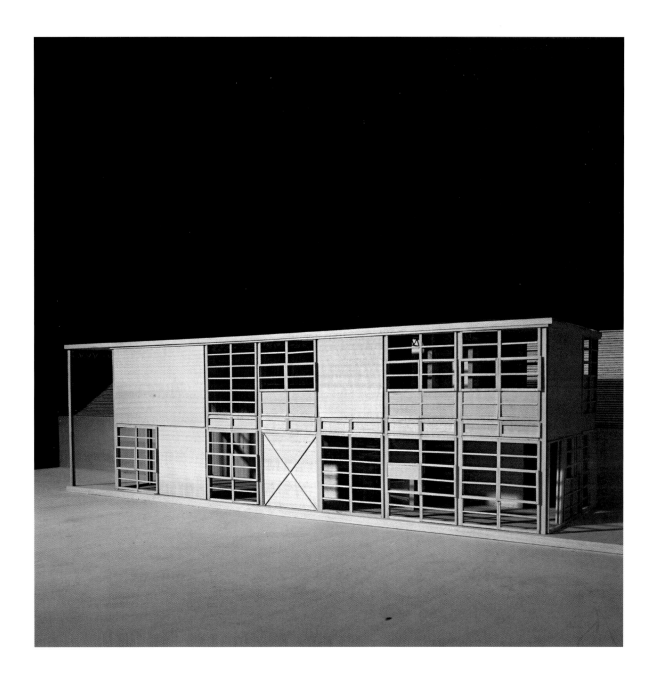

Le Corbusier
Chapelle Notre-Dame-du-Haut, Ronchamp, 1954

»Formen unter dem Licht. Drinnen und draußen; darunter und darüber. Drinnen: man tritt ein, man geht umher, man schaut beim Gehen, und die Formen erklären sich, entwickeln sich, fügen sich zusammen. Man ist unaufhörlich verschiedenen und sukzessiven Erschütterungen ausgesetzt. Und dann offenbart sich das Spiel, das gespielt wird. Man geht umher, man bewegt sich, man hört nicht auf, sich zu bewegen, sich zu drehen.«

Le Corbusier: *Konferenz in der Reale Accademia d'Italia. Die Tendenzen der Rationalistischen Architektur in Verbindung mit der Malerei und der Bildhauerei.* Rom 1936.

»Der Schlüssel
Das ist Licht und das Licht erhellt Formen

Und diese Formen haben Gewalt, zu erregen
durch das Spiel der Proportionen

durch das Spiel der Beziehungen
der unerwarteten, verblüffenden

Aber auch durch das geistige Spiel
ihres Grundes zu sein:
ihre wahrhaftige Geburt,
ihre Fähigkeit zu dauern,
Struktur,

Beweglichkeit, Kühnheit, ja Tollkühnheit, Spiel – von Geschöpfen, die die wesentlichen Geschöpfe sind – die Grundlage der Architektur.«

Le Corbusier: *Ronchamp.* Stuttgart 1957.

"Forms under light. Inside and outside, above and below. Inside: one enters, one walks around, one looks around while walking, and the forms explain themselves, develop, blend together. Time and again one is subjected to various and successive shocks. And then the game being played becomes apparent. You walk about, you keep moving and turning around. Note what sort of apparatus man responds to architecture with."

Le Corbusier: *Konferenz in der Reale Accademia d'Italia. Die Tendenzen der Rationalistischen Architektur in Verbindung mit der Malerei und der Bildhauerei.* Rome 1936.

"The key is light
and light illuminates shapes

and shapes have emotional power.
By the play of proportions

by the play of relationships
unexpected, amazing.

But also by the intellectual play
of purpose:
their authentic origin,
their capacity to endure,
structure,

astuteness, boldness, even temerity, the play
of those vital abstractions which are the essential qualities
the components of architecture."

Le Corbusier: *Ronchamp.* Stuttgart 1957.

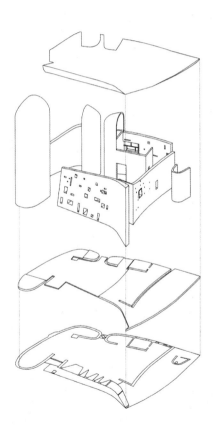
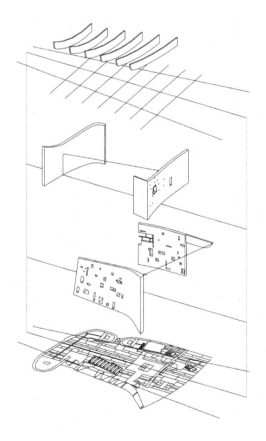

| Raumbildung | Spatial definition | Raumstruktur | Spatial structure |
| Körper und Raum | Objects and space | Form und Ordnung | Form and order |

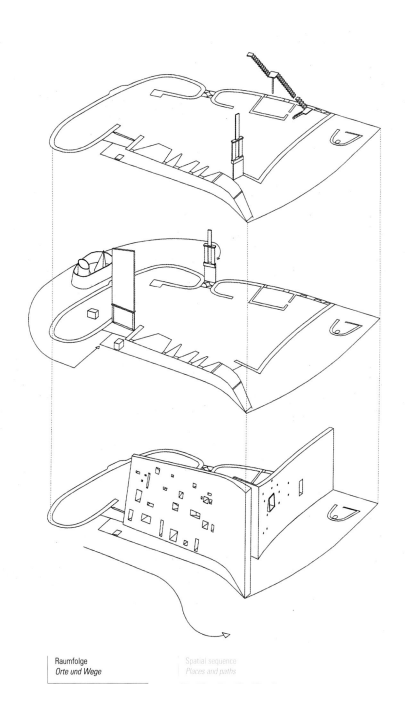

Raumfolge
Orte und Wege

Spatial sequence
Places and paths

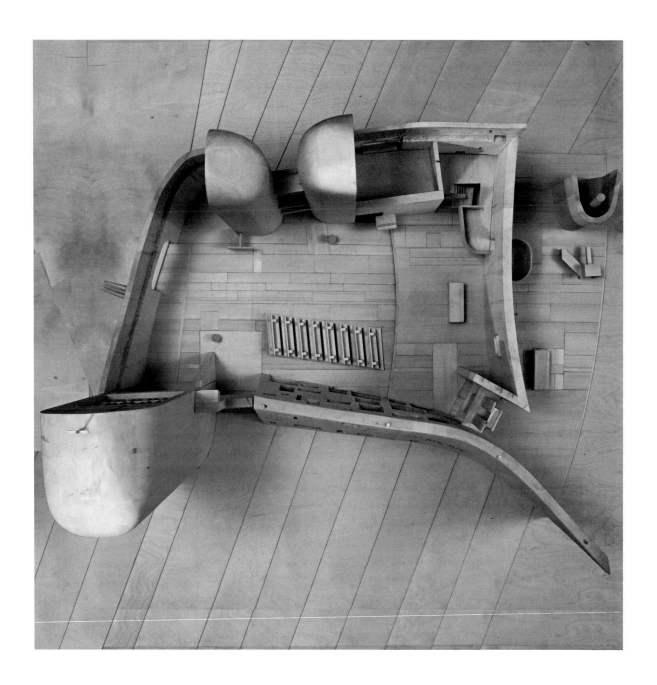

113

Carlo Scarpa
Olivetti Showroom, Venedig, Venice, 1958

»Bauen in einem definierten Kontext erleichtert meist die Arbeit. Nehmen wir zum Beispiel den Showroom von Olivetti. Er besteht aus einem vorderen und einem rückwärtigen Bereich, die durch eine Wand getrennt sind. Außerdem musste ein oberes Geschoss erschlossen werden; es gab Räume, die nicht verändert werden konnten, einen zentralen Pfeiler, zwei Fenster – wo sollte die Treppe verlaufen? Ich musste auch Teile zerstören. Dadurch dass ich die Treppe an einem komplizierten Ort vorgesehen hatte, konnte ich auch Substanz entfernen – und mir war daran gelegen, Dinge loszuwerden. So konnte ich nämlich die Länge besser ausnutzen. (…) Die Treppe war wirklich teuer. Ich fragte meinen Kunden, ›Was möchten Sie? Soll ich Ihnen einen Büroraum entwerfen?‹ – ›Nein, nein – eine Visitenkarte.‹«

Scarpa, Carlo: *Tausend Zypressen*. Vortrag in Madrid 1978.
In: Scarpa, Carlo: *The complete works*. Mailand 1987.

»Im Grunde genommen bin ich byzantinisch. Kann Architektur Poesie sein? Frank Lloyd Wright hat diese Frage In einer Vorlesung in London bejaht. Ich würde dagegen behaupten: nicht immer. Man kann nicht ein Stück poetische Architektur entwerfen. Die Poesie liegt in den Dingen selber.«

Scarpa, Carlo: *Can architecture be poetry?* Ebenda.

"When the context is fixed, perhaps it makes the work easier. Take an example, the Olivetti showroom. It consisted of a front section and then, after a wall, there was another area. You had to go to the floor above; there were spaces you couldn't change, a central pillar, two windows – where should the stairs go? I even had to violate things. By putting in the most difficult point I could throw something out – and I was interested in getting rid of things. In this way I could make better use of the length. Once the problem is grasped you get to work – the staircase isn't bad at all, it's made of juxtaposed blocks of marble. It's a really expensive staircase. I asked my client, 'What do you want? Do I have to design office space?' – 'No, no – a visiting-card.'"

Scarpa, Carlo: *Tausend Zypressen*. Lecture in Madrid 1978.
In: Scarpa, Carlo: *The complete works*. Milan 1987.

"Essentially I'm a Byzantine. Can architecture be poetry? Certainly. Frank Lloyd Wright said so in a lecture in London. But not all the time: architecture is only sometimes poetry. You mustn't think, 'I'll produce a poetic piece of architecture.' Poetry is born of the thing itself."

Scarpa, Carlo: Can architecture be poetry? Ibid.

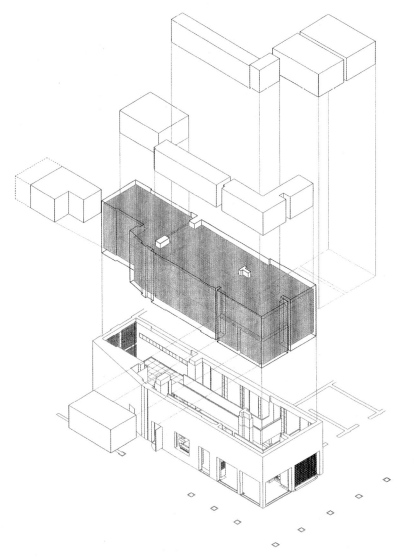

Raumbildung
Körper und Raum

Spatial definition
Objects and space

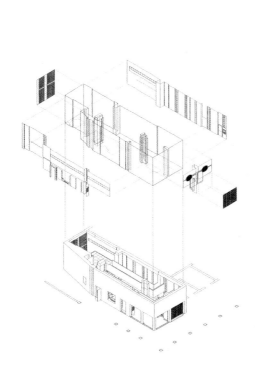
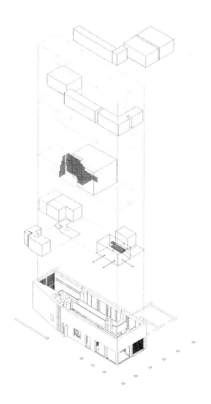

Raumgestalt
Material, Farbe, Licht

Spatial design
Material, color, light

Raumfunktion
Raum und Nutzung

Spatial function
Space and use

Robert Venturi
Haus für Vanna Venturi, House for Vanna Venturi, Chestnut Hill, 1964

»Das Haus ist zugleich komplex und einfach, offen und geschlossen, groß und klein, seine Anordnung vereinigt die typischen Elemente eines Hauses im Allgemeinen und die diesem Haus eigenen Elemente im Speziellen. Sowohl außen wie innen ist es ein kleines Haus mit großzügigem Maßstab. Der Hauptgrund für diesen großen Maßstab war, ein Gegengewicht zu der Komplexität des Hauses zu schaffen. Komplexität in Verbindung mit kleinen Elementen in kleinen Gebäuden bedeutet Spannung.

Zwei senkrechte Elemente – der offene Kamin und die Treppe wetteifern um die zentrale Lage. Die äußere Form ist einfach und einheitlich und repräsentiert den Maßstab eines üblichen Hauses. Die Fassade mit ihrer konventionellen Anordnung von Tür, Fenster, Schornstein und Giebel bildet das fast symbolische Bild eines Hauses. Die architektonische Vielfalt im Inneren des Hauses spiegelt sich jedoch auch an dessen Äußerem wider. Die unterschiedliche Anordnung der Fenster, ihre Größen und Formen, die Durchbrüche in den Außenwänden, wie auch der aus der Mitte seitlich verschobene Kamin stehen in einem Widerspruch zur Symmetrie der äußeren Form.«

Venturi, Robert: *Erläuterungsbericht zum Vanna Venturi Haus*. In: Sanmartin, A. (Hg.): *Venturi, Rauch & Scott Brown. Bauten und Projekte/Works and Projects*. Stuttgart 1986.

"This building is both complex and simple, open and closed, big and little; its order accommodates the generic elements of the house in general, and the circumstantial elements of a house in particular. The main reason for the large scale is to counterbalance the complexity. Complexity in combination with scale in small buildings means busyness. The plan is symmetric, yet this symmetry is distorted to accommodate to the particular needs of the spaces.

Two vertical elements – the fireplace-chimney and the stair – compete, as it were, for central position. The outside form – as represented by the parapeted wall and the gable roof – is simple and consistent: it represents this house's public scale. The front, in its conventional combinations of door, windows, chimney and gable, creates an almost symbolic image of a house. The architectural complexities inside are reflected on the outside. The varying locations and sizes and shapes of the windows and perforations on the outside walls, as well as the off-center location of the chimney, contradict the overall symmetry of the outside form."

Venturi, Robert: *Erläuterungsbericht zum Vanna Venturi Haus*. In: Sanmartin, A. (Ed.): *Venturi, Rauch & Scott Brown. Bauten und Projekte/Works and Projects*. Stuttgart 1986.

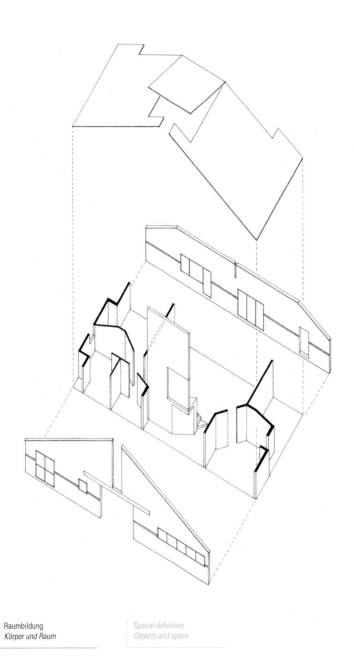

Raumbildung
Körper und Raum

Spatial definition
Objects and space

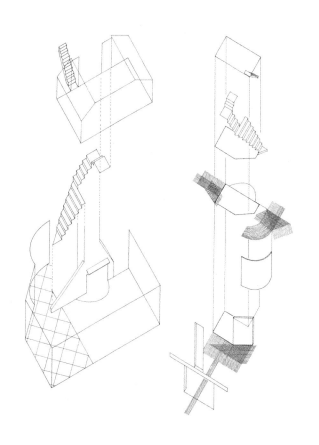
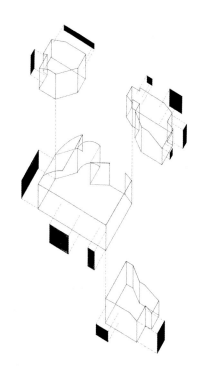

Raumfolge
Orte und Wege

Spatial sequence
Places and paths

Raumgestalt
Material, Farbe, Licht

Spatial design
Material, color, light

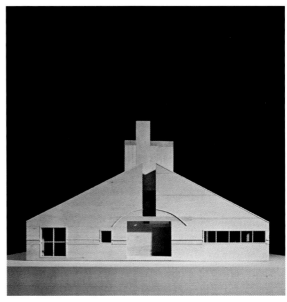

Herman Hertzberger
Centraal Beheer, Apeldoorn, 1972

»Raumgliederung war das Prinzip, das dem Entwurf vom Centraal Beheer-Verwaltungsgebäude zugrunde liegt. Es wurde davon ausgegangen, dass Arbeit und Erholung weder individuell noch kollektiv, sondern in kleinen Gruppen stattfindet. Die Untersuchung der Lage zeigte, dass alle Komponenten des Programmes als 3 × 3 Meter große Räume oder Plätze interpretiert werden können, die eine multiple Grundeinheit bilden. Anstatt eines riesigen kompakten Volumens entstand durch die Auflösung in mehr oder weniger selbständige, durch passagenähnliche Galerien getrennte, kleinere Blöcke eine aus mehreren Komponenten zusammengesetzte Konfiguration. Da es in dem Komplex überall Ein- und Ausgänge gibt, erinnert dieser eher an ein städtisches Ensemble als an ein Einzelgebäude, oder, noch treffender, an eine Art Siedlung. Beim Centraal Beheer ist die erstaunliche Wirkung, die die Mitarbeiter der Firma erzielten, als sie ihre Arbeitsplätze einrichteten und ihnen durch die Wahl der Farbe, die Aufstellung von Topfpflanzen und anderen Gegenständen eine persönliche Note verliehen, nicht allein darauf zurückzuführen, dass die Ausstattung des Inneren bewusst den Benutzern des Gebäudes überlassen wurde. Die Form des Raumes selbst – mit den Einbauten und Zusatzeinrichtungen – muss den Benutzern die Möglichkeit bieten, ihre Arbeitsplätze ihren persönlichen Wünschen und Bedürfnissen entsprechend auszustatten.«

Hertzberger, Herman: *Vom Bauen – Vorlesungen über Architektur.* München 1995.

"The articulation of space was the principle underlying the design of the Centraal Beheer insurance office. The point of departure was the tenet that all work, as well as all recreational activity, takes place in small groups, not individually but not collectively either. A study of the situation showed that all the different components in the programme could be interpreted as spaces, or places, of 3 × 3 meters, or of multiples thereof. Instead of a single colossal constructed volume, a more transparent conglomerate of numerous small components was achieved, thanks to the differentiation into more or less independent small blocks separated by arcade-like passages. And since there are entrances and exits throughout the complex, it looks more like a piece of a city than like a single building – most of all it resembles a kind of settlement. The surprising effect obtained by the people who work at Central Beheer in the way they had arranged and personalized their office spaces with colors of their own choice, potted plants and objects they are fond of is not merely the logical consequence of the fact that the interior finishing was deliberately left to the users of the building. The form of the space itself must offer the opportunities, including basic fittings and attachments etc., for the users to fill the spaces according to their personal needs and desires."

Hertzberger, Herman: *Lessons for Students in Architecture.* Rotterdam 1991.

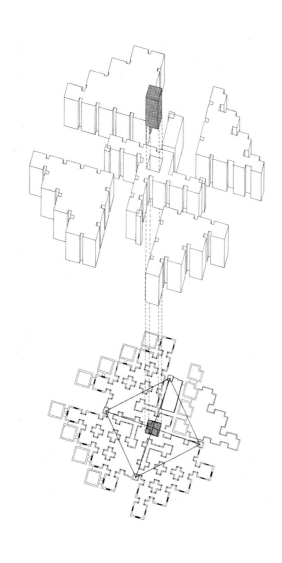
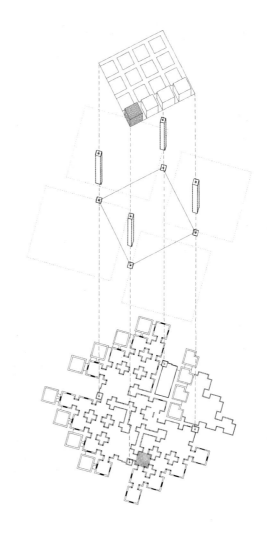

| Raumbildung | Spatial definition | Raumstruktur | Spatial structure |
| Körper und Raum | Objects and space | Form und Ordnung | Form and order |

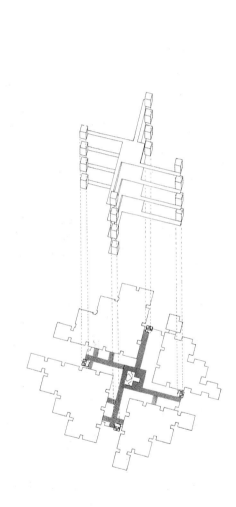

Raumfolge
Orte und Wege

Spatial sequence
Places and paths

Raumgestalt
Material, Farbe, Licht

Spatial design
Material, color, light

Mario Botta
Casa Bianchi, Riva San Vitale, 1973

»In diesem Fall war das Baugrundstück stark abschüssig. Bei derartigen Geländeverhältnissen ist offenkundig ein mehrgeschossiger Bau erforderlich. Die Raumgliederung sieht die Verteilung der einzelnen funktionalen Bereiche auf mehrere Geschosse vor. Mit seinem kompakten Volumen antwortet dieses Wohngebäude in besonderer Weise auf die Beschaffenheit des Geländes und schlägt in einem extensiv bebauten Kontext eine bauliche Verdichtung mit mehreren Geschossen vor. Was verstehen wir heute unter einem Haus?

Ich halte es zum Beispiel für wichtig, dass Wohnhäuser ihre ursprüngliche Bedeutung zurückerlangen. Sie sollen sich wie das Haus Adams präsentieren und eindringlich von unserem ›Schutzbedürfnis‹ sprechen. Das Haus ist also im Unterbewusstsein der Ort geblieben, wo sich der Mensch erholen kann, wo er sich selbst findet, seine Geschichte und Erinnerung zurückgewinnt und träumen kann. Andererseits ist es ebenso wichtig, darauf hinzuweisen, dass sich der Innenraum in den Außenraum verlängern sollte (der Ausgang der Höhle). Die Seitenwände sind es, die den Innen- vom Außenraum trennen, und sie sollen wie Schutzwände wirken. Der Raum wird auf diese Weise zum Mikrokosmos zwischen Himmel und Erde und bezieht auch den Makrokosmos ein, der zum lebendigen Bestandteil des Hauses wird.«

Botta, Mario: *Das Haus – Ethik des Bauens*. Basel 1997.

"In this case I was given the brief of building a house on a steeply sloping site. Obviously, a site of this sort calls for construction on several levels. With its compact volume, the house is a specific response to the nature of the site, and suggests a practical multilevel typology for a densely-built area. But it also implies a particular concept of a house. What is a house today? What role should it fulfill?

For example, I think it's important that the primeval significance of the home should be restored: the home should once again be 'Adam's house', in the sense that it should convey very powerfully the primal need for shelter and protection. In our subconscious mind, the house has remained the place where we go to recharge our batteries, to feel ourselves again, to review our lives and memories, to give free rein to our imagination. On the other hand, it is equally important that the interior space projects outwards to the exterior (the mouth of the cave). A wall is a fine thing indeed if it gives you the feeling of being protected. In this way, interior living space becomes a microcosm between the earth and the sky, so that features of the cosmos like the horizon, the solar cycle, the moon and the stars play an active role in the life of the house."

Botta, Mario: *Das Haus – Ethik des Bauens*. Basel 1997.

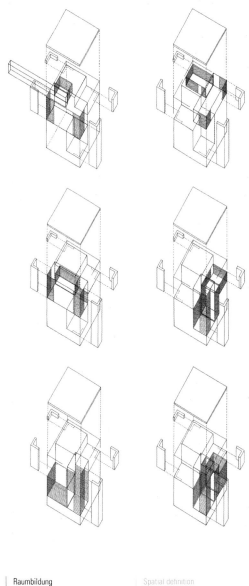

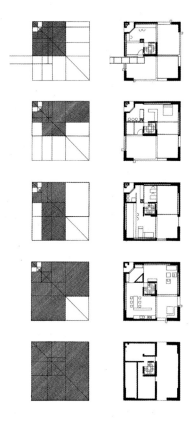

Raumbildung
Körper und Raum

Spatial definition
Objects and space

Raumfunktion
Raum und Nutzung

Spatial function
Space and use

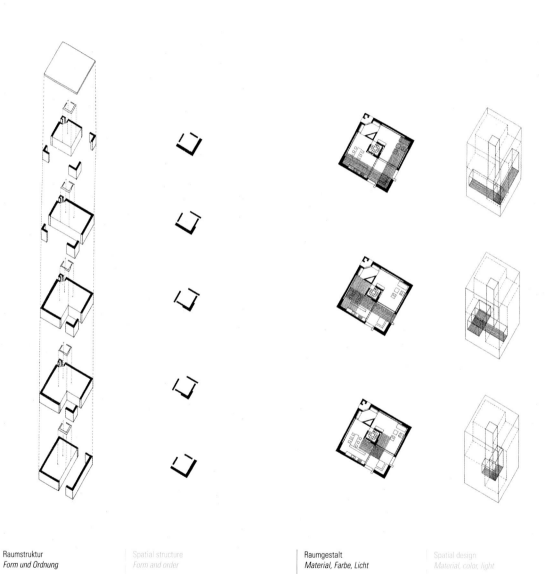

| Raumstruktur | Spatial structure | Raumgestalt | Spatial design |
| *Form und Ordnung* | *Form and order* | *Material, Farbe, Licht* | *Material, color, light* |

 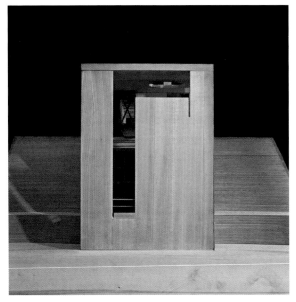

Mario Campi, Franco Pessina
Casa Felder, Lugano, 1973

»Erste Forderung gegenüber einer Aufgabe ist nicht die Anwendung eines bestimmten Stils, sondern die Formulierung und die entwerferische Entwicklung eines architektonischen Themas, d. h. die Fähigkeit, die vielschichtigen Bedingungen einer Aufgabe unter einem kohärenten Blickwinkel zu ordnen. Realismus in der Arbeit bedeutet nicht Pragmatismus. Realismus ist eine Denkweise, die den Entwurf als eine mögliche Wirklichkeit, als physisches Objekt begreift, das in einer kulturellen Situation auf einen konkreten Ort ausgerichtet ist. Wenn ich diese Kriterien gedanklich zusammenfasse, so wird deutlich, dass mich an der Architektur weniger der Stil als vielmehr die Struktur interessiert. Es interessiert mich jene Haltung, die das architektonische Thema, die angestrebte Reduktion, durch alle Ebenen des Entwurfs hindurch konsequent, kohärent, ökonomisch, diszipliniert, rational und realistisch überprüft und verfolgt. Nur dadurch erzeugt man, nebst der Gewissheit und der zum Entwerfen benötigten Überzeugung, auch jene Ungewissheit, die den Raum für die architektonische Spekulation offen lässt.«

Campi, Mario. In: Feireiss, Kristin (Hg.): *Mario Campi Franco Pessina. Bauten und Projekte Buildings and Projects.* Berlin 1994.

"The first demand made by a task is not the application of a specific style but the formulation and the designing development of an architectural subject; this means the ability to organize the complex conditions of the task from a coherent point of view. Realism at work does not mean pragmatism. Realism is a method which understands the design as a possible reality, as a physical object which is oriented towards a concrete place in a cultural context. As I now summarize these criteria, it becomes clear that what interests me in architecture is less the style than the structure. I'm interested in the approach which consistently, coherently, economically, rationally, realistically and with discipline examines and keeps track of the architectural subject, the desired reduction throughout all the levels of the design. I think that only in so doing does one create, in addition to the certainty and the conviction needed for designing, the uncertainty which provides room for architectural speculation."

Campi, Mario. In: Feireiss, Kristin (Ed.): *Mario Campi Franco Pessina. Bauten und Projekte Buildings and Projects.* Berlin 1994.

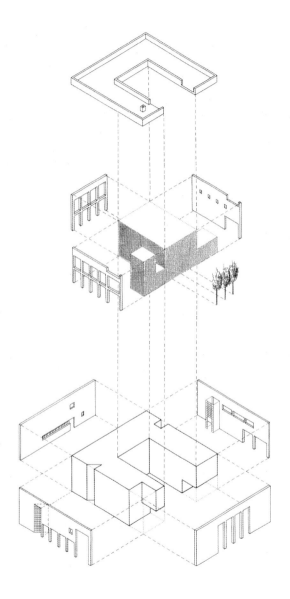

Raumbildung
Körper und Raum

Spatial definition
Objects and space

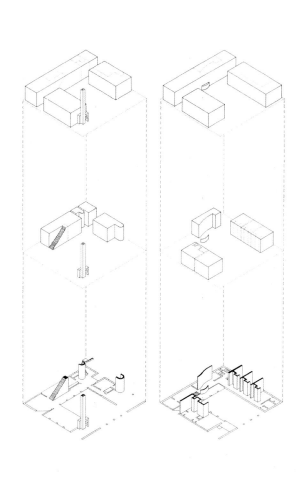
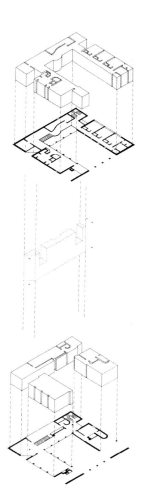

| Raumfolge | Spatial sequence | Raumfunktion | Spatial function |
| Orte und Wege | Places and paths | Raum und Nutzung | Space and use |

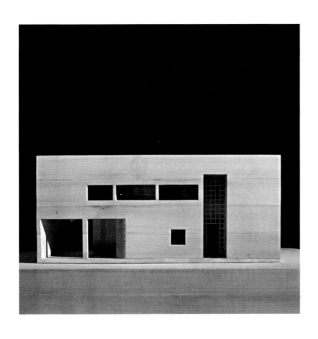 

Louis I. Kahn
Yale Center for British Art, New Haven, 1977

»Konstruktion ist Entwerfen mit Licht. Die Konstruktion bestimmt das Licht. Sie ist die Möglichkeit, Licht zu gewinnen. Und daraus folgt doch, dass ich diese Möglichkeit verliere, wenn ich die Konstruktion verstecke. Ich finde, natürliches Licht gibt einem Zimmer sein Wesen, seinen Charakter, seine Stimmung. Ich empfinde die Tatsache viel stärker, dass der Raum sichtbar machen muss, wie er entstanden ist. An diesem Punkt öffnet sich das Gemüt dem Wesen der Räume selbst. Raum ist nicht Raum, wenn man nicht klar erkennen kann, wie er gemacht wurde.«

Kahn, Louis I.: Klotz, H.; Cook, J. W.: *Architektur im Widerspruch*. Zürich 1981.

»Im Yale Center for British Art versuchte ich, diesen einen Punkt noch weiter hervorzuheben. Sie [die Technik des Gebäudes] soll aus einem anderen Material sein als das Gebäude, sie hat nichts mit dem Gebäude an sich zu tun. Es ist der Raum, der wichtig ist, wenn man in ihm steht. Das ganze Gebäude bedeutet nichts im Vergleich zu dem Raum, in dem man sich befindet. Der Raum ist der Beginn der Architektur.«

Kahn, Louis I.; Wurman, Richard Saul: *What will be has always been. The words of Louis I. Kahn*. New York 1986.

"Construction is designing with light. The structure determines the light. It is the possibility of giving light. And from this it follows that I lose this possibility if I hide the construction. I think natural light gives a room its essence, its character, its mood. We are very different [referring to Mies]. I feel far more strongly that a room must show how it came to be. At this point your mind opens to the essence of the rooms themselves. A room is not a room if one cannot clearly see how it was made."

Kahn, Louis I.: Klotz, H.; Cook, J. W.: *Architektur im Widerspruch*. Zurich 1981.

"In the Yale Center for British Art I tried to develop this point further. They [the technical aspects of the building] should be made of a different material than the building. They have nothing to do with the building itself. The room is what is important when you stand in it. The whole structure means nothing compared to the space in which one finds oneself. The room is the beginning of architecture."

Kahn, Louis I.; Wurman, Richard Saul: *What will be has always been. The words of Louis I. Kahn*. New York 1986.

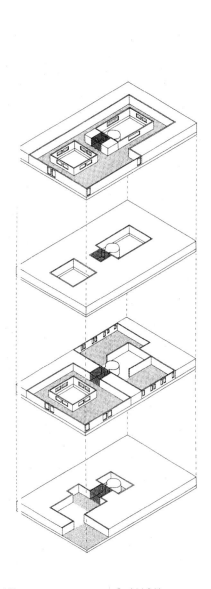
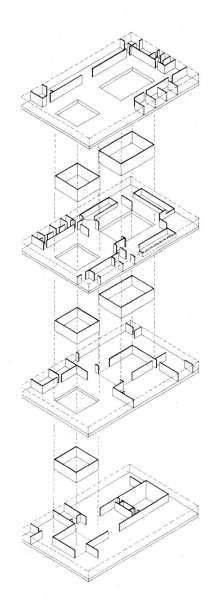

| Raumbildung | Spatial definition | Raumstruktur | Spatial structure |
| Körper und Raum | Objects and space | Form und Ordnung | Form and order |

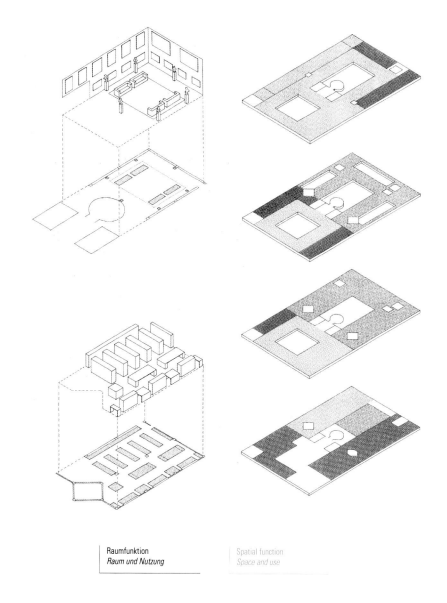

Raumfunktion
Raum und Nutzung

Spatial function
Space and use

147

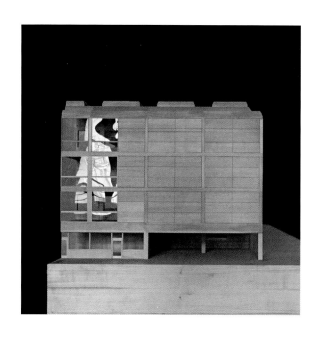

Tadao Ando
Haus Koshino, Koshino House, Ashiya, 1981

»Die Spannung in der Architektur liegt in dieser Konfrontation von Innenraum und Außenraum. Folglich ist der Bereich, in dem Innen und Außen aufeinandertreffen, nämlich die Öffnung, von entscheidender Bedeutung. In meinen Häusern spielt die Wand eine trennende und eine verbindende Rolle. Die amorphen und immateriellen Elemente Wind, Licht, Himmel und Landschaft werden ausgeschnitten und von der Wand, als Verbindung zum Innenraum, vereinnahmt. Damit werden sie Teil des architektonischen Raumes. In diesem Moment verliert das Objekt seine Bestimmung und offenbart seinen individuellen und ursprünglichen Charakter. Je strenger eine Wand ist, desto mehr spricht sie zu uns. Sie ist wie ein Spiegel, in dem sich Landschaft und Licht abbilden. Je nach Situation streicht das Licht weich an einer Kurve entlang oder fällt in hartem Kontrast auf eine dunkle Fläche.«

Ando, Tadao: *Buildings, Projects and Writings*. New York 1984.

»So wie ich ihn verwende, verliert Beton seine skulpturale Form und seine Schwere. Seine Aufgabe ist es, Licht und gleichmäßige Oberflächen zu schaffen. Beton ist hier ein kaltes, anorganisches Material, mit gewisser Strenge. Ich möchte auch gar nicht die Natur eines Materials an sich ausdrücken, ich benutze die Eigenschaft eines Materials zum Ausdruck eines Raumes. Die Wand hört auf zu existieren, der Bewohner spürt nur den ihn umgebenden Raum.«

Ando, Tadao: *Complete Works*. London 1995.

"In architecture this tension signifies an intense confrontation between the inside and the outside. Thus, those places where the internal order meets the external order, that is, the areas of fenestration in a building, are of extreme importance. In my buildings, walls play a dual role, serving both to reject and affirm. The amorphous and immaterial elements of wind, sunlight, sky and landscape are cut out and appropriated by walls which serve as agents of the internal world. These elements are assimilated as aspects of the architectural space. In that tense moment, an object loses its definition and its individual and basic character becomes manifest. The more austere a wall is, the more it speaks to us. At times it is a mirror in which landscapes and light are dimly reflected. Light that diffuses around a corner and gathers in the general darkness contrasts strongly with direct light."

Ando, Tadao: *Buildings, Projects and Writings*. New York 1984.

"The way I employ it, concrete lacks sculpturesque solidity and weight. It serves to produce light, homogeneous surfaces. I treat concrete as a cold, inorganic material with a concealed background of strength. My intent is not to express the nature of the material itself but to employ it to establish the single intent of the space. The actual walls cease to exist, and the body of the beholders is aware only of the surrounding space."

Ando, Tadao: *Complete Works*. London 1995.

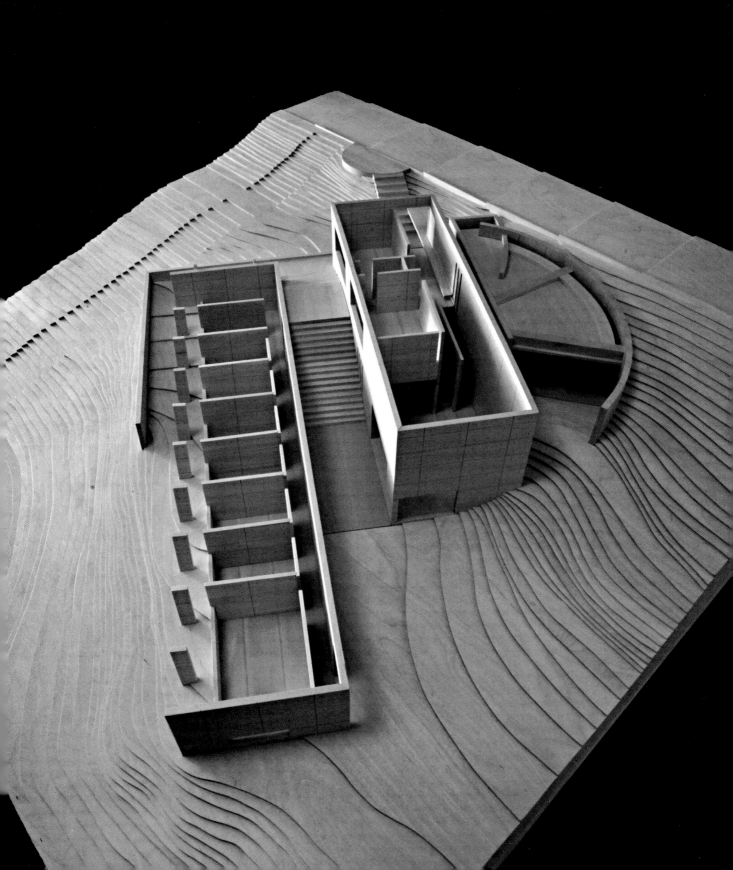

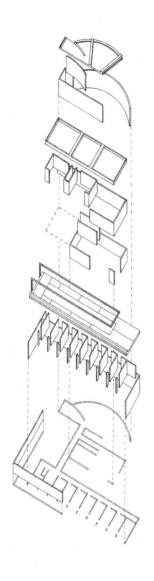
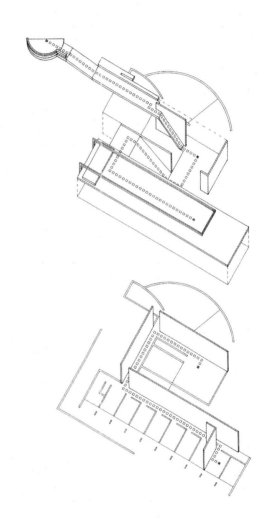

Raumbildung
Körper und Raum
Spatial definition
Objects and space

Raumfolge
Orte und Wege
Spatial sequence
Places and paths

| Raumgestalt | Spatial design |
| Material, Farbe, Licht | Material, color, light |

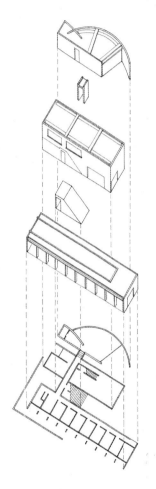

| Raumfunktion | Spatial function |
| Raum und Nutzung | Space and use |

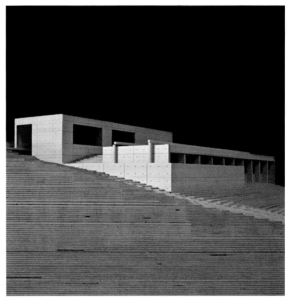

Christian de Portzamparc
Café Beaubourg, Paris, 1986

»Schließlich bin ich mir darüber klar geworden, dass man im Grunde genommen, ohne es zu wollen, immer wieder an dem gleichen Projekt arbeitet. Was im Café Beaubourg zählt, das sind die Leute, das ist das Leben ringsum.«

De Portzamparc, Christian. In: Aslan, Carlo; Dru, Line: *Cafés – Restaurants*. Stuttgart 1991.

»Ein Raum, in dem man sich bewegen kann, ohne sich festgehalten zu fühlen.«

»Jedes Objekt, jede Form ist alternativ Objekt oder Kontext, Form oder Grund, immer im Austausch mit anderen Objekten.«

Jacques, Michel (Hg.): *Christian de Portzamparc*. Berlin 1996.

"In the end it became clear to me that we generally, without wanting to, work on the same project again and again. When it comes to Café Beaubourg, what's important is the people, the life all around."

De Portzamparc, Christian. In: Aslan, Carlo; Dru, Line: *Cafés – Restaurants*. Stuttgart 1991.

"[A] room in which one can move without feeling contained."

"Every object, every form alternates between object and context, figure and ground, in continuous interchange with other objects."

Jacques, Michel (Ed.): *Christian de Portzamparc*. Berlin 1996.

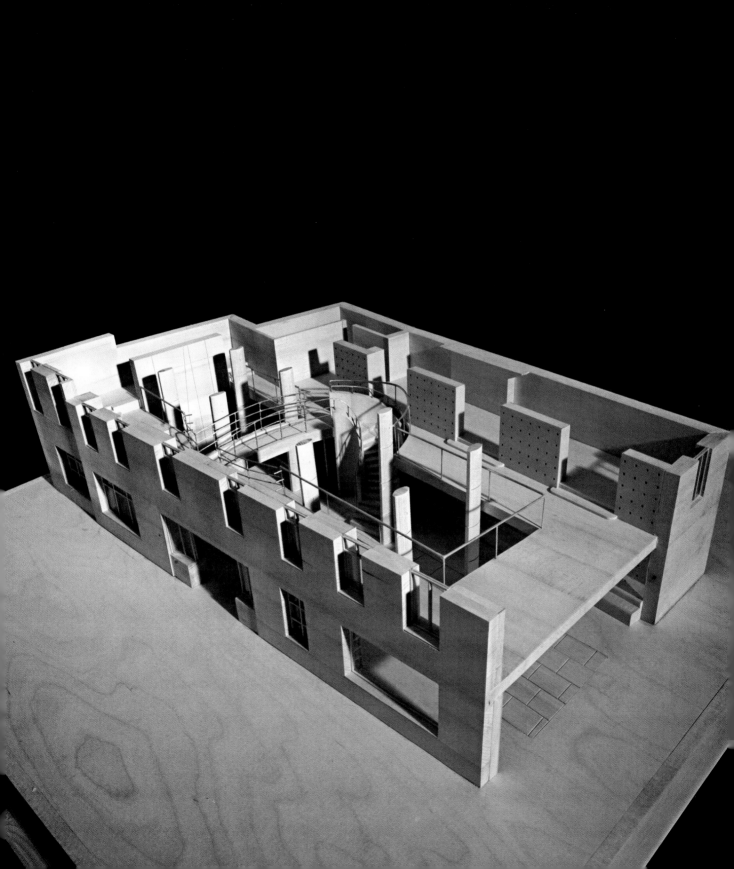

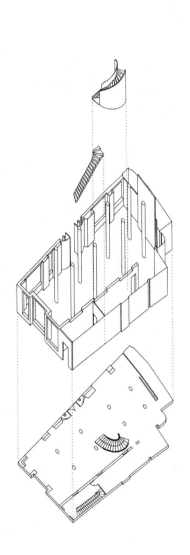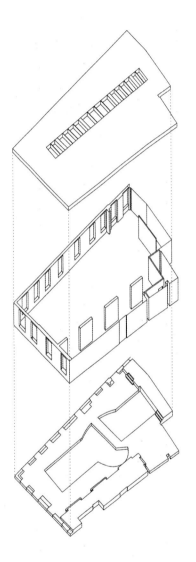

Raumbildung
Körper und Raum

Spatial definition
Objects and space

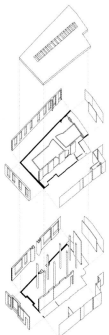

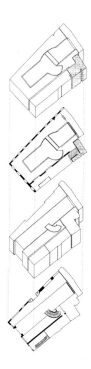

Raumstruktur
Form und Ordnung

Spatial structure
Form and order

Raumfunktion
Raum und Nutzung

Spatial function
Space and use

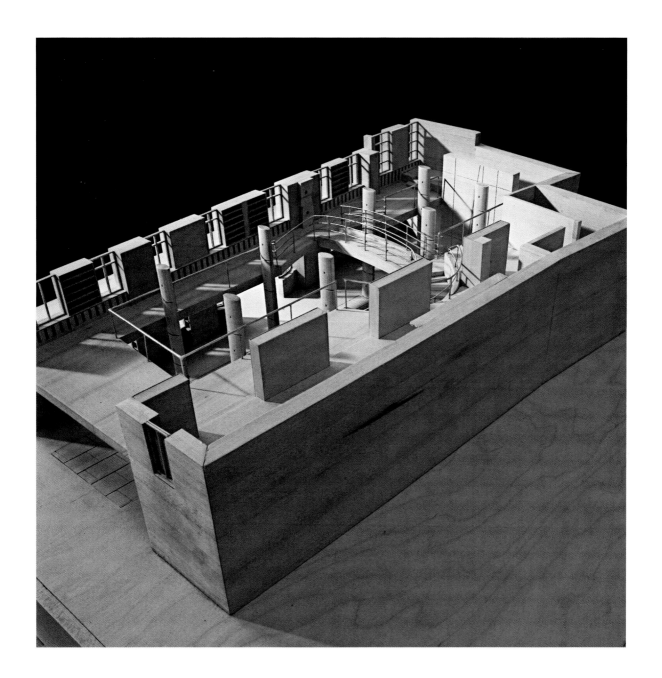

Günther Domenig
Steinhaus, Steindorf, 1986

»Die Architektur und die Landschaft
Die Architektur und der Ort
Die Architektur und die Idee
Der eine Ort
Bewuchs und Stein
Der andere Ort
Offen und weich
Die subjektiven Dimensionen des Ortes
Der Ort als Erinnerung
Der Ort als Erfahrung
Der Ort als Darstellung
Der Ort als Selbstdarstellung«

»Aus dem Boden wachsen Hügel aus denen die Felsen brechen. Sie sind durch die Schlucht getrennt. Die Felsen aus Metall und die Hügel aus Mauern sind durchdrungen von Räumen und Wegen die unter das Wasser reichen. Im tiefen Keller die Stufenspirale der Pfeil und das Wasser aus der Erde im stehenden und in den schwebenden Felsen träumt man auch im Huckepack. In der Schlucht wandert man im Würfel trifft man sich, im Keil isst man. Der tiefe Weg unter das Wasser. Vom Aufbruch auf Abruf zum Durchbruch.«

Domenig, Günther; Raja, Raffaele:
Werkbuch. Wien 1991.

"Architecture and the landscape
Architecture and the site
Architecture and an idea
The one site
Grass and stone
The other site
Open and soft
The subjective dimension of the site
The site as memory
The site as experience
The site as representation
The site as self-projection"

"Hills rise from the ground
rocks protruding
separated by the abyss
the rocks of metal

The hills of walls
are filled
with rooms and paths
reaching under the water

In the deep cellar
the spiral staircase
the arrow
and the water emerging from
the ground

In the standing
and in the suspended rock
dreams also
come piggyback

The abyss is where we walk
the cube where we meet
the wedge where we eat

The low path under the water
from an emergence
on request
to a breakthrough"

Domenig, Günther; Raja, Raffaele:
Werkbuch. Vienna 1991.

Raumstruktur
Form und Ordnung

Spatial structure
Form and order

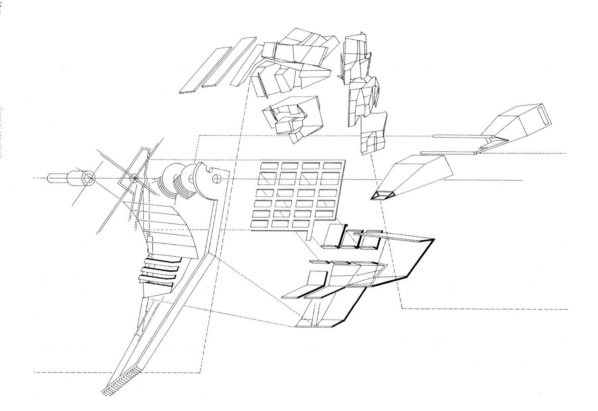

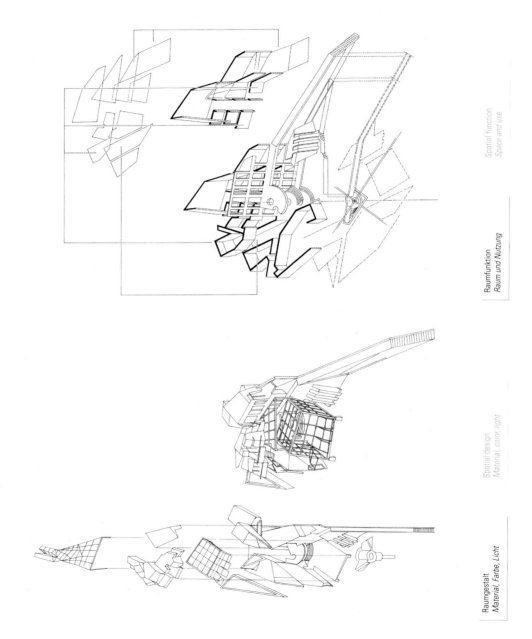

Raumfunktion
Raum und Nutzung
Spatial function
Space and use

Spatial design
Material, color, light

Raumgestalt
Material, Farbe, Licht

165

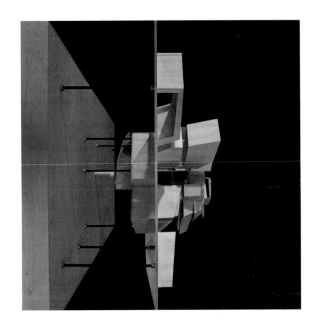
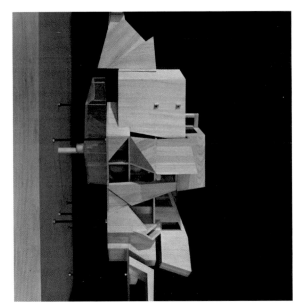

Zaha Hadid
Werksfeuerwehr, Vitra Fire Station, Weil am Rhein, 1993

»Zu dem Entwurf des Hauses gelangten wir auf Umwegen, weil wir nicht damit begannen, das Gebäude an sich zu entwerfen, sondern wir entwickelten es in Hinblick auf die gesamte Umgebung, wir positionierten es, und dann erst nahm es Gestalt an. Wir kamen sozusagen durch die Hintertür. Zu Beginn gab es die Wandscheiben, die so zueinander gestellt wurden, dass sich zwischen ihnen Enge und Weite entwickelte; Expansion und Rückzug. So gab es eine Verlagerung aus der Fläche zum Körper und die Wände, nun nicht mehr zweidimensional, wurden körperhaft. Aus dem Spiel mit den Linien wurde ein Zusammenspiel der Volumen, die sich miteinander verwoben. Der Grundgedanke war, den Raum so fließend wie möglich zu gestalten. Wir haben verschiedene Möglichkeiten und Bedingungen untersucht. Wie mit einer Linse haben wir uns der Situation genähert oder Abstand genommen. Auf seine Art funktioniert das Haus genauso, physisch und visuell. Der Wunsch nach einem in höchstem Maße wandelbaren Raum war gegenwärtig – Innenraum und Außenraum, in Verbindung mit absoluter Leichtigkeit. Leichtigkeit verleiht man einer Masse nicht durch das Material, sondern durch die Geometrie des Gebäudes.«

Hadid, Zaha. In: Futagawa, Yukio (Hg.): *GA Document Extra 03. Zaha M. Hadid.* Tokio 1995.

"We arrived at our design for the building by an indirect route, as we didn't begin by designing the building as an isolated object but rather developed it in the context of the whole site; only when we had positioned it did it begin to take shape. You could say we came in through the back door. We started off by making a series of walls, between which big spaces and small spaces could be made, expansion and retraction. Eventually there was a shift from planes to volumes and the walls became much more volumetric. It became more than just a play of lines, but sort of a play of volumes and how they start to weave into each other. The intention was to keep the space as fluid as possible. We did many studies on the various possibilities and conditions. Then we began to focus and zoom into the site like a lens. In a way the building does that too. The building kind of expands and contracts in both ways. Physically in some ways and visually in others. There was always this desire to have a highly transformable space – interior and exterior, combined with absolute lightness and ease. You don't impart lightness to an object by changing the material. You achieve it through the geometry of the building."

Hadid, Zaha. In: Futagawa, Yukio (Ed.): *GA Document Extra 03. Zaha M. Hadid.* Tokyo 1995.

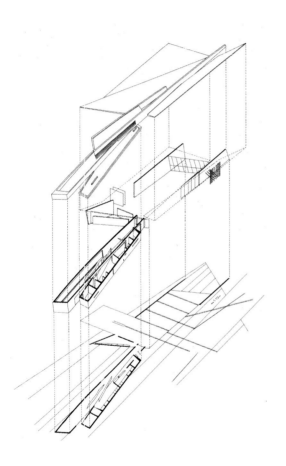

Raumbildung
Körper und Raum

Spatial definition
Objects and space

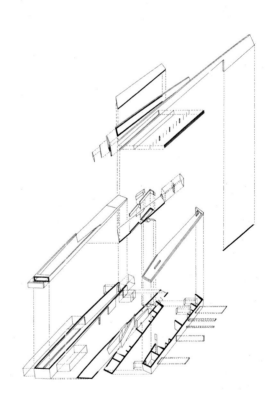

Raumstruktur
Form und Ordnung

Spatial structure
Form and order

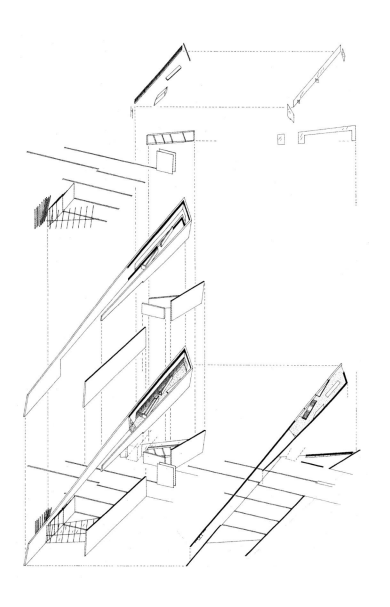

Raumgestalt
Material, Farbe, Licht

Spatial design
Material, color, light

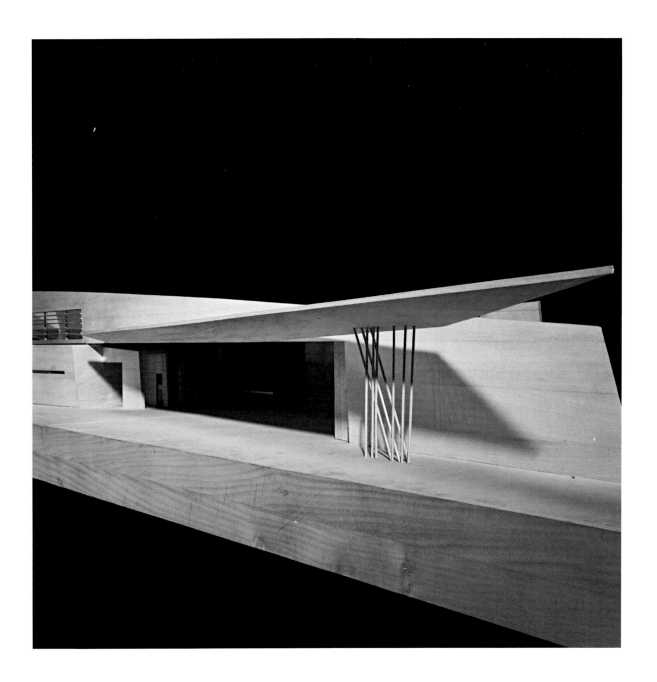

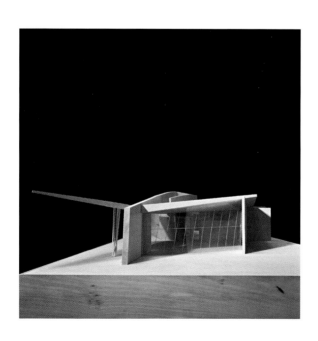

Peter Zumthor
Therme Vals, 1996

»Berg, Stein, Wasser – Bauen im Stein, Bauen mit Stein, in den Berg hinein bauen, aus dem Berg heraus bauen, im Berg drinnen sein –, wie lassen sich die Bedeutungen und die Sinnlichkeit, die in der Verbindung dieser Wörter steckt, architektonisch interpretieren, in Architektur umsetzen? Entlang diesen Fragestellungen haben wir das Bauwerk entworfen, hat es Schritt für Schritt Gestalt angenommen.

In der Art eines rechtwinklig ausgelegten Höhlensystems mäandriert ein zusammenhängender Innenraum durch die aus großen freistehenden Steinblöcken bestehende Grundstruktur des Bades. Dieses Raumkontinuum entwickelt sich von intimen und abgedunkelten Raumpassagen auf der Bergseite, durch die man das Bad betritt, zu immer größer werdenden Hohlräumen, die nach vorne ans Tageslicht und zur Aussicht führen. Der Außenraum dringt hier in das Gebäude ein. Die großartige Landschaft des gegenüberliegenden Talhanges, architektonisch gerahmt in riesigen Bildern, strömt ins Innere.

Von außen betrachtet erscheint das Gebäude als Ganzes wie ein großer, durchlöcherter Stein. Präzise geschnitten dort, wo dieser mächtige ›Stein‹ aus der Hangkante herausragt, wird die angeschnittene Struktur des Steines zur Fassade. Und dieser ›Stein‹ ist aus Stein gebaut. Eine durchgehende Schichtenfolge aus Natursteinen; Valser Gneisplatten, in vielen Lagen geschichtet, abgebaut im etwas weiter taleinwärts gelegenen Steinbruch, bestimmen Schnitt und Aufriss.«

Zumthor, Peter: *Therme Vals*. Zürich 2007.

"Mountain, stone, water, building in stone, building with stone, building into the mountain, building out of the mountain, being inside the mountain – our attempts to give this chain of words an architectural interpretation, to translate into architecture its meanings and sensuousness, guided our design for the building and step by step gave it form.

In the manner of a geometric cave system, the continuous internal space meanders through the vast free-standing blocks of stone that comprise the basic structure of the baths. This continuum of spaces develops from intimate and dimly-lit passage spaces on the mountain side of the building, where one enters, to larger and larger caverns that lead toward daylight and the view out. Here, the outside world penetrates into the building. The fantastic scenery of the slope on the other side of the valley, architecturally framed in huge pictures, streams inside.

Viewed from without, the building as a whole resembles a large porous stone. At the points where this 'large stone' projects out of the slope, the precisely cut cavern structure becomes façade. And this stone is built of stone. The section and profile of the structure as a whole are determined by a continuous series of natural stone strata – layer upon layer of Vals gneiss, quarried somewhat further up the valley."

Zumthor, Peter: *Therme Vals*. Zurich 2007.

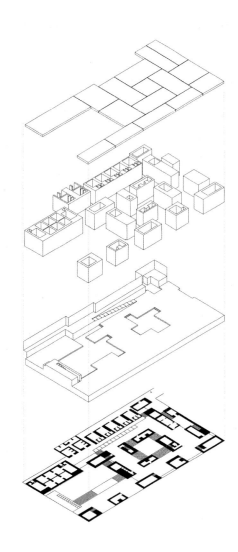

Raumbildung
Körper und Raum

Spatial definition
Objects and space

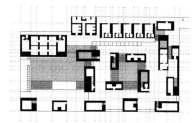
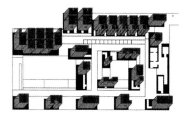

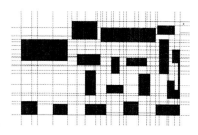
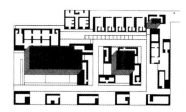

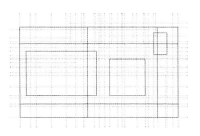
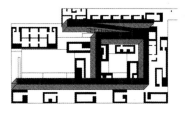

Raumstruktur
Form und Ordnung

Spatial structure
Form and order

Raumfolge
Orte und Wege

Spatial sequence
Places and paths

UNStudio van Berkel & Bos
Möbius-Haus, Moebius House, Het Gooi, 1998

»In maximaler Ausdehnung, die es dennoch nicht zu kompakter oder übergroßer Gestalt steigert, vermag das Haus vom Innern her, die Vorstellung einer Wanderung durch die Landschaft wachzurufen. Die Gestalt des Möbius-Hauses ist in ihrer räumlichen Qualität im Grundriss wie im Schnitt gegenwärtig und überträgt einen 24-Stunden-Zyklus aus Schlafen, Arbeiten und Wohnen ins Innere. Wie sich Inneres wiederum nach außen wendet, so folgt auch die Form diesen Übergängen; verglaste Partien und Teile der Betonkonstruktion tauschen die Rollen, wo Glasfassaden vor jene Konstruktion treten, Trennwände aus Glas bestehen und Gegenstände der Inneneinrichtung wie Tische und Treppen aus Beton sind.«

Van Berkel, Ben; Feireiss, Kristin (Hg.): *Mobile Forces – Mobile Kräfte*. Berlin 1994.

"By being stretched to a maximum rather than displaying a compact or tall shape, the house conveys from the interior the idea of a walk in the countryside. The Moebius loop, the spatial quality of which means that it is present in both plan and section, translates into the interior a 24-hour cycle of sleeping, working and living. As the loop turns inside out, the materialization follows these changeovers; glazed details and concrete structural elements swap roles as glazed façades are put in front of the concrete construction, dividing walls are made of glass and furniture such as tables and stairs are made of concrete."

Van Berkel, Ben; Feireiss, Kristin (Ed.): *Mobile Forces – Mobile Kräfte*. Berlin 1994.

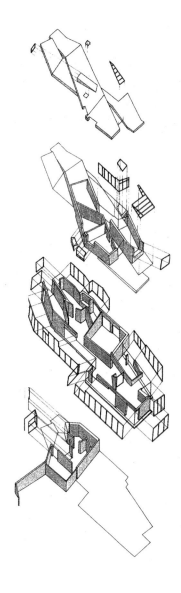
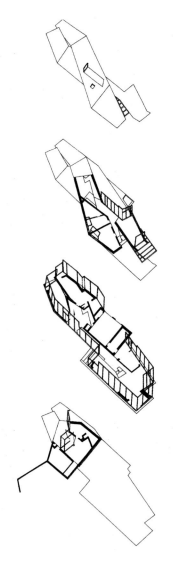

| Raumstruktur | Spatial structure | Raumgestalt | Spatial design |
| Form und Ordnung | Form and order | Material, Farbe, Licht | Material, color, light |

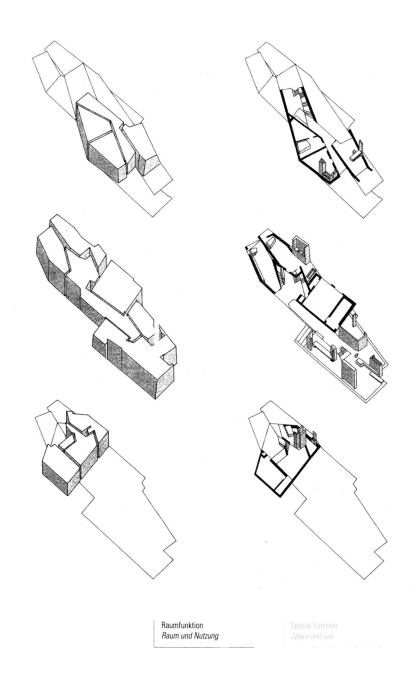

Raumfunktion
Raum und Nutzung

Spatial function
Space and use

Axel Schultes, Charlotte Frank
Krematorium, Berlin, 1998

»Was not tut, um diesem Uneigentlichen in der Architektur beizukommen, nach 400 Jahren Postrenaissance und der Hoffnung der Moderne, ist eine Morphologie, eine Dramaturgie des Raumes, die das Streben nach Gestalt auf die Entwicklung neuer Räume und Raumtypen wendet – mit der verwegenen Hoffnung, eine neue, uralte Konvention, einen architektonischen Imperativ herauszubilden. ›Alles ist Raum‹, sagen die Modernsten – und machen damit unsere Kunst zum Kunstgewerbe. ›Schönes in dieser schönen Arbeit‹ ist nur zu leisten in der präzisen Abgrenzung von Raum durch die Schwere des Materials und beseelt durch das Licht.«

Schultes, Axel; Frank, Charlotte: *Axel Schultes in Bangert, Jansen, Scholz, Schultes: Projekte / Projects 1985–1991*. Berlin 1992.

»Einen Ort der Ruhe, einen Raum der Stille, der das Vergängliche und das Endgültige des Ereignisses ausbalanciert, das Schwere deutlich und das Leichte möglich macht.«

Schultes, Axel: *Krematorium Baumschulenweg*. In: *Architektur Aktuell*. Nummer 223. 1998.

"What we need in order to come to terms with these improprieties in architecture, after 400 years of the post-Renaissance and the hopes of modernism, is a morphology – a dramaturgy – of space, one that focuses the quest for form on the development of new spaces and new types of rooms, with the audacious hope of evolving a new, age-old convention, an architectural imperative. 'Everything is space', claims a self-appointed avant-garde, equating our architectural art with decorative craft. We can only create 'beauty with this beautiful vocation' by using the weight of matter as a precise delineation of space and inspiring life into it with light."

Schultes, Axel; Frank, Charlotte: *Axel Schultes in Bangert, Jansen, Scholz, Schultes: Projekte / Projects 1985–1991*. Berlin 1992.

"A place of rest, a space for silence that balances the ephemerality and the finality of the moment, which makes heaviness clear and lightness possible."

Schultes, Axel: *Krematorium Baumschulenweg*. In: *Architektur Aktuell*. Number 223. 1998.

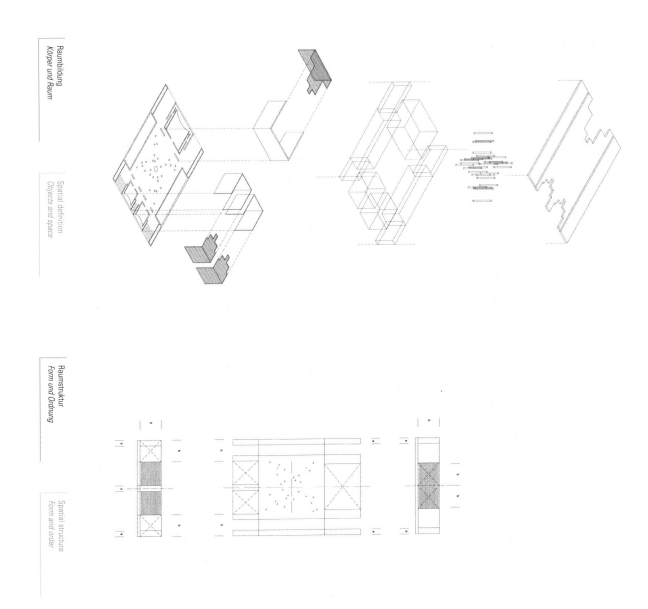

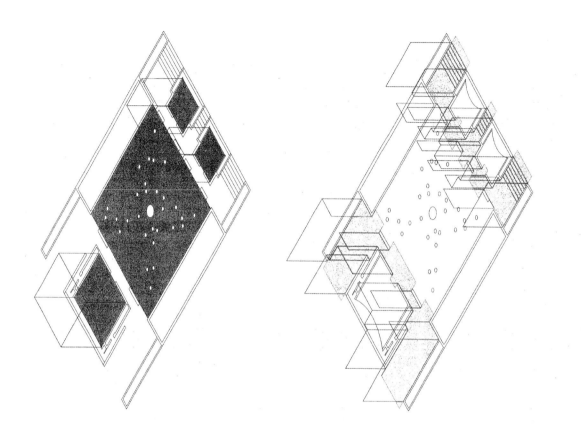

Raumfolge
Orte und Wege

Spatial sequence
Places and paths

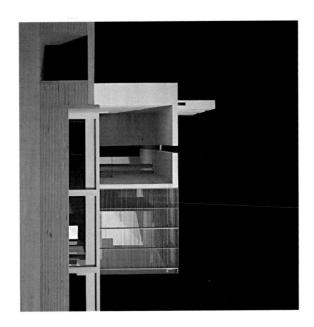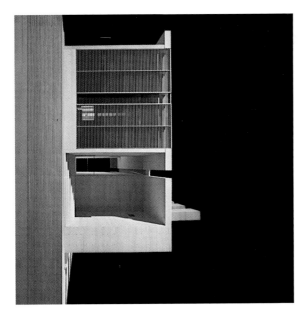

Rem Koolhaas
Maison à Bordeaux, 1998

»Dann hatte der Ehemann einen Autounfall. Er wäre beinahe gestorben, aber er überlebte. Jetzt sitzt er im Rollstuhl.«

»Der Architekt entwarf ein Haus – oder genauer drei Häuser übereinander. Das untere war höhlenartig – eine Reihe von Höhlen, die für das privateste Familienleben aus dem Hügel heraus gemeißelt wurden. Das oberste Haus war in ein Haus für das Ehepaar und in ein Haus für die Kinder unterteilt. Das wichtigste Haus lag, fast unsichtbar, dazwischen – zur Hälfte innen, zur Hälfte außen. Der Mann hatte seinen eigenen ›Raum‹ oder vielmehr eine ›Station‹: Einen Aufzug, 3 × 3,5 Meter, der sich frei zwischen den Häusern bewegte. Wenn er an einer Etage ›andockte‹ oder darüber schwebte, veränderte er den Plan und das Schauspiel. Eine einzige ›Mauer‹ neben dem Fahrstuhl durchschnitt jedes Haus. Sie enthielt alles, was der Ehemann brauchen könnte Bücher, Kunstschätze und im Keller Wein. Die Bewegung des Fahrstuhls veränderte jedes Mal die Architektur des Hauses. Eine Maschine war dessen Herz.«

Koolhaas, Rem: *Maison à Floirac*. In: *ARCH+*. Nummer 132. 1998.

"Suddenly, the husband had a car accident and almost lost his life. Now he needs a wheelchair."

"The architect designed a house – or better three houses on top of each other. The lowest part was a series of cave-like spaces carved out of the hill for the most intimate life of the family. The 'top house' had separate areas for the husband and wife and for the children. The most important house was located, almost invisible, in the middle – half inside, half outside. The husband had his own 'room' or rather 'station': an elevator, 3 × 3.5 meters, which moved freely between the levels of the house. When it 'docked' at a level or was suspended above one, the layout and the pageantry changed. A single 'wall' next to the elevator intersected each house. It held everything the husband could want – books, art treasures and, in the cellar, wine. Each movement of the lift changed the architecture of the house. A machine was at its heart."

Koolhaas, Rem: *Maison à Floirac*. In: *ARCH+*. Number 132. 1998.

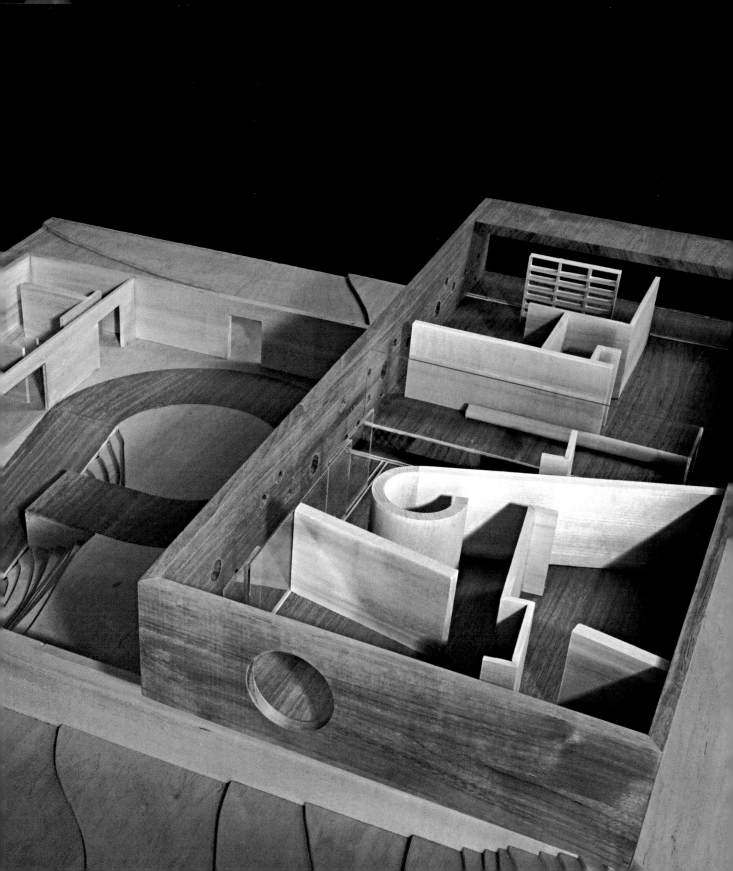

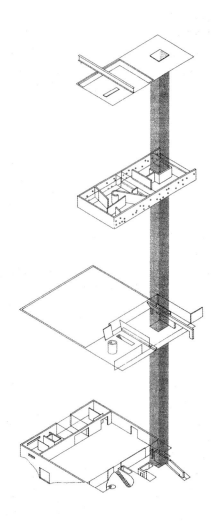

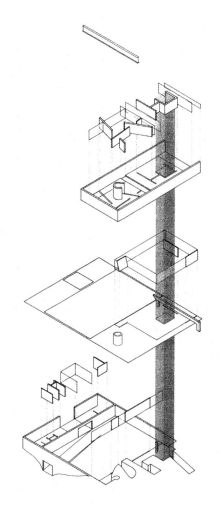

Raumbildung
Körper und Raum

Spatial definition
Objects and space

Raumstruktur
Form und Ordnung

Spatial structure
Form and order

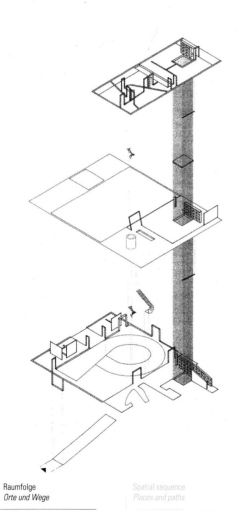

Raumfolge
Orte und Wege

Spatial sequence
Places and paths

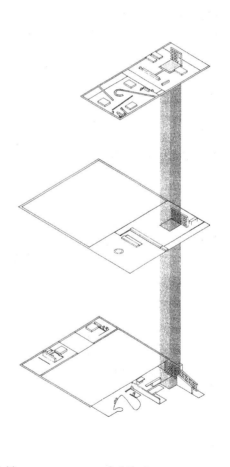

Raumfunktion
Raum und Nutzung

Spatial function
Space and use

 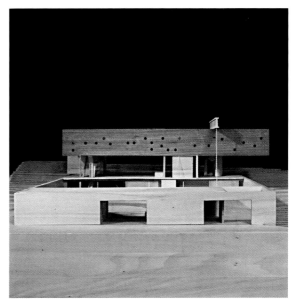

William Alsop
Peckham Library, London, 1999

»Eine Bibliothek ist irgendwie ein altmodischer Begriff, der, im Zeitalter des Internets, von CD-ROM, Fax, elektronischer Post, TV, Videos, Hörbüchern und darstellenden Künsten, irgendwie überflüssig erscheint. Warum, um Himmels Willen, sollte jemand so ein Bauwerk errichten wollen? (…) Schweigen (…) bei unserer neuen Bibliothek für Peckham geht es um Lärm. Sie will da sein! Der Ort, den der Londoner Bezirk Southwark und wir gerade kreieren, ist ein Brennpunkt für die Interessen und Werte der Leute, ein Treffpunkt/ein Debattierort/ein Lernort/eine Ruhezone/mitten im Lärm des Zentrums. Dieses Gebäude ist da, um Freude zu bereiten.«

Alsop, William: *Will Alsop. 1990–2000*. London 2002.

"A library is somehow an old-fashioned term, which, in the age of the Internet, CD-ROM, fax, electronic mail, TV, videos, talking books and performing arts, seems somehow redundant. Why on earth would someone want to build such an edifice? (…) silence (…) our new library for Peckham is about noise! It wants to be there. The place that the London Borough of Southwark and ourselves is creating is a focal point for peoples' concerns and values, a meeting place/a debating place/a learning place/a peaceful place/amidst the noise of the centre town. This building is there to be enjoyed."

Alsop, William: *Will Alsop. 1990–2000*. London 2002.

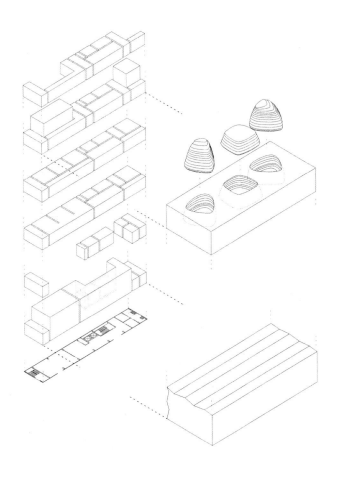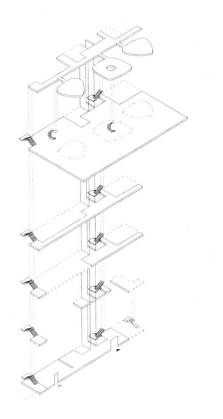

| Raumbildung | Spatial definition | Raumfolge | Spatial sequence |
| Körper und Raum | Objects and space | Orte und Wege | Places and paths |

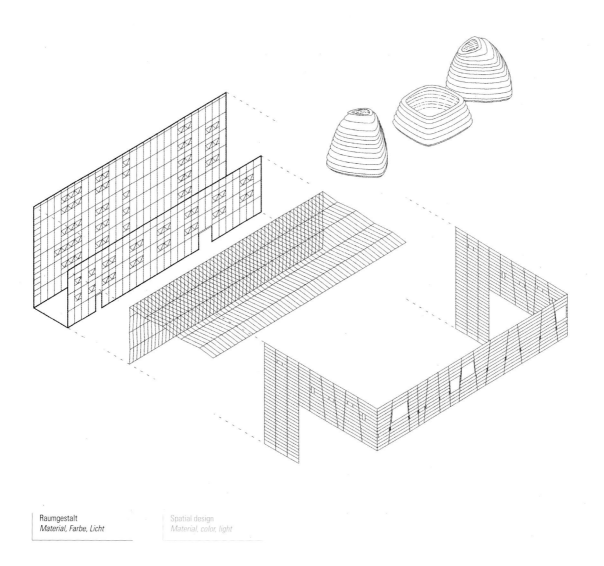

Raumgestalt
Material, Farbe, Licht

Spatial design
Material, color, light

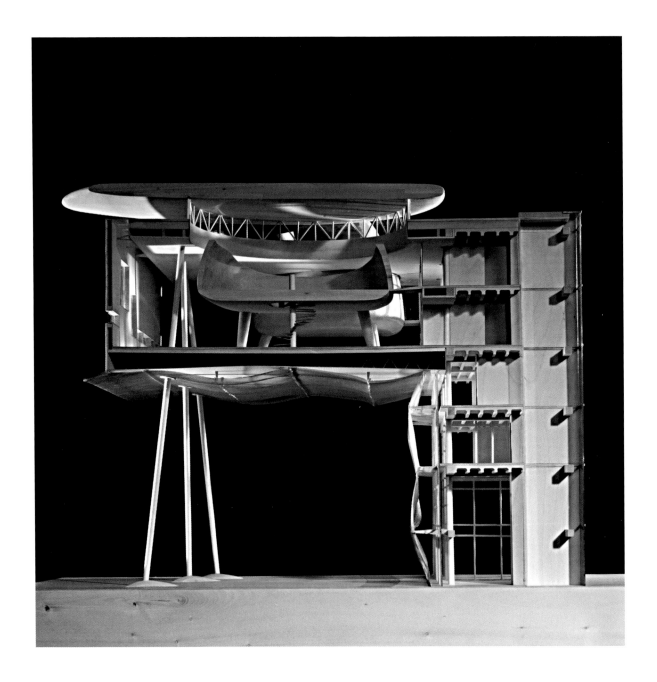

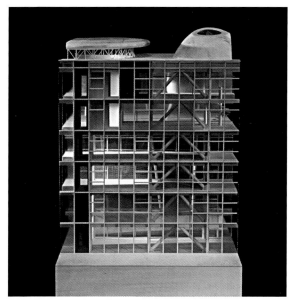

203

Peter Zumthor
Schweizer Pavillon, Hannover, Hanover, 2000

»Die Architektur kennt zwei grundsätzliche Möglichkeiten der Raumbildung: den geschlossenen Körper, der in seinem Innern Raum isoliert, und den offenen Körper, der einen mit dem unendlichen Kontinuum verbundenen Raumteil umschließt. Die Ausdehnung des Raumes kann durch offen in die Tiefe des Raumes gesetzte oder gereihte Körper wie Platten oder Stäbe sichtbar gemacht werden. Ich nehme nicht in Anspruch zu wissen, was Raum wirklich bedeutet. Je länger ich über das Wesen des Raumes nachdenke, desto geheimnisvoller erscheint er mir. Eines jedoch weiß ich bestimmt: Wenn wir uns als Architekten mit dem Raum beschäftigen, dann befassen wir uns lediglich mit einem kleinen Teil dieser Unendlichkeit, die die Erde umgibt. aber jedes Bauwerk bezeichnet einen Ort in dieser Unendlichkeit.

Gebäude, die uns beeindrucken, vermitteln uns immer ein starkes Gefühl für ihren Raum. Sie umschließen diese geheimnisvolle Leere, die wir Raum nennen.«

Zumthor, Peter: *Architektur denken*. Baden 1998.

"In architecture there are two basic possibilities for spatial composition: the closed architectural body which isolates space within itself and the open body which embraces an area of space that is connected with the endless continuum. The extension of space can be made visible through bodies such as slabs or poles placed freely or in rows in the spatial expanse of a room. I do not claim to know what space really is. The longer I think about it, the more mysterious it becomes. About one thing, however, I am sure: when we, as architects, are concerned with space, we are concerned with but a tiny part of the infinity that surrounds the earth, but each building marks a unique place in this infinity.

Buildings that have a strong impact always convey an intense feeling of their spatial quality. They embrace the mysterious void we call space in a special way and make it vibrate."

Zumthor, Peter: *Thinking Architecture*. Basel/Boston 1999.

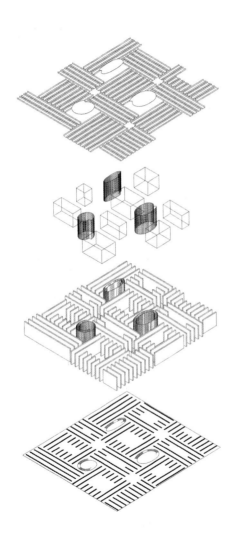

| Raumbildung | Spatial definition |
| Körper und Raum | Objects and space |

| Raumgestalt | Spatial design |
| Material, Farbe, Licht | Material, color, light |

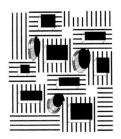
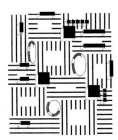

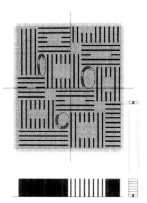
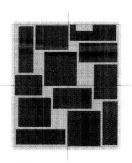
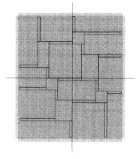

Raumfolge
Orte und Wege

Spatial sequence
Places and paths

Raumstruktur
Form und Ordnung

Spatial structure
Form and order

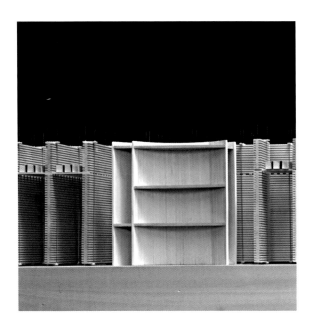

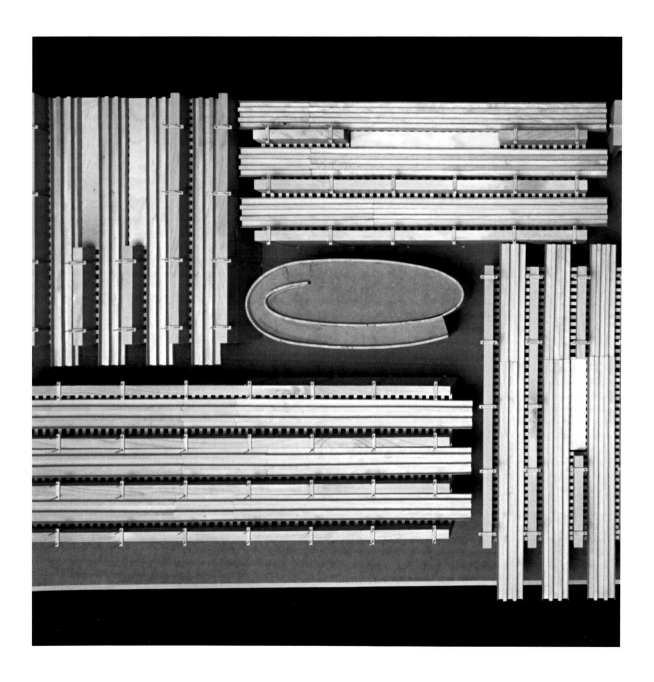

Frank O. Gehry
DZ Bank AG, Berlin, 2001

»Der Pferdekopf für das Büro- und Wohngebäude am Pariser Platz entsprang dem Peter Lewis Haus. Dass der nach Berlin gekommen ist, lag daran, dass wir uns einen Entwurf für das Atrium ausgedacht hatten mit dem Konferenzzentrum in der Mitte. Viele Architekten haben so etwas gemacht. Es ist keine originelle Strategie, aber was Beruhigendes, eine nette Strategie. Ich fing an, mit dem Raum zu spielen und ich stellte fest, dass ich es nicht rechtzeitig lösen kann. Ich hatte hier diese schöne Pferdekopfform und sie funktionierte, also hab ich sie angepasst und gesagt: ›Wir ändern sie später, die werden sie nicht mögen, aber wir haben etwas und es wird fertig aussehen.‹ Also haben wir sie eingereicht und die haben sie geliebt, wir haben den Wettbewerb gewonnen. Ich bin dabei geblieben, denn auch ich hab sie geliebt. Ich denke, da hatte Claus Sluter großen Einfluss.«

Gehry, Frank O.: *Gehry Talks: Architecture + Process*. New York 1999.

"The horse's head for the Pariser Platz mixed-use building, part commercial, part residential, came from the Peter Lewis house. The reason it got to Berlin is that we came up with a plan for the atrium with the conference center in the middle – an obvious scheme. A lot of architects have done that. It's not a very original strategy, but it's a comforting thing, a nice strategy. I started to play with the space, and I realized I couldn't solve it in time for the competition. I had this beautiful horse-head shape here and it worked, so I adapted it and said, 'We'll change it later, they're not going to like it, but at least it's a finished thing and it will look finished.' So we put it in and they loved it, and we won the competition. I stuck with it and refined it, because I loved it, too. I think that Claus Sluter was a big influence there."

Gehry, Frank O.: *Gehry Talks: Architecture + Process*. New York 1999.

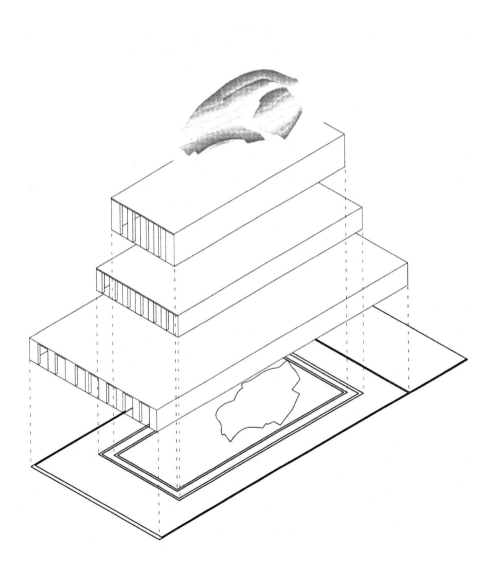

Raumbildung
Körper und Raum

Spatial definition
Objects and space

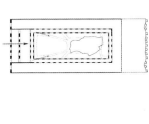
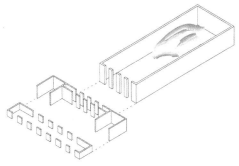
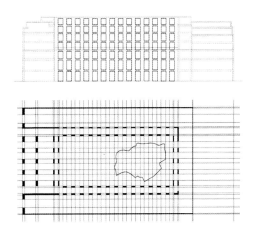

| Raumfolge | Spatial sequence | Raumstruktur | Spatial structure |
| *Orte und Wege* | *Places and paths* | *Form und Ordnung* | *Form and order* |

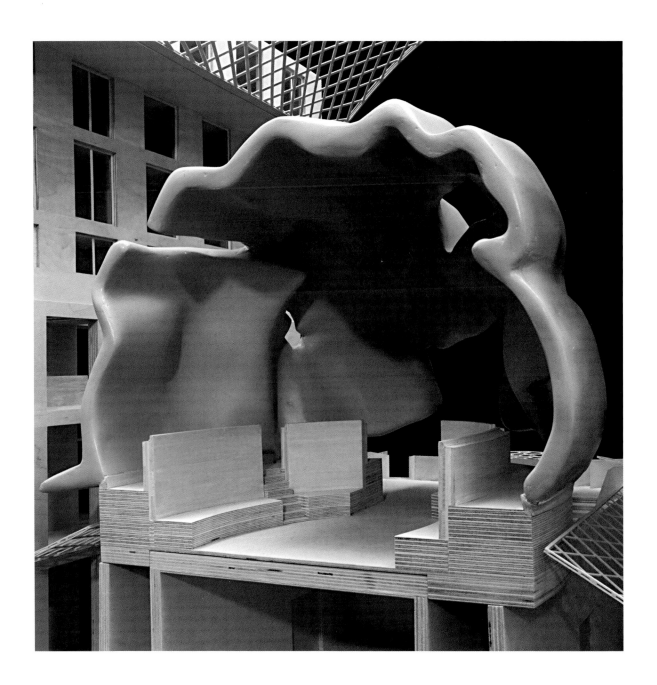

Register

Frank Lloyd Wright
Unity Temple
Chicago, 1907

Eckhard Breilmann (Modellbau)
Oliver Burk, Matthias Gühne (Zeichnungen)

Frank Lloyd Wright
Haus für Frederick C. Robie
Chicago, 1910

*Mario Anschütz, Ilka Hausmann, Michael Rohner,
Sandra Wiedemann* (Modellbau und Zeichnungen)

Robert van 't Hoff
Villa Henny
Utrecht, 1919

Sabrina Colombo, Loris Negro (Modellbau)
Claudia Lübbe (Zeichnungen)

Theo van Doesburg, Cornelis van Eesteren
Maison Particulière
Paris, 1923

Jonas Jüttner, Jan Schneidewind
(Modellbau und Zeichnungen)

Gerrit T. Rietveld
Haus Schröder
Utrecht, 1924

Julia Brinkmann, Sabine Kamke, Arne Mailbohm (Modellbau)
Virginijus Gerdvilis (Zeichnungen)

Le Corbusier
Pavillon de L'Esprit Nouveau
Paris, 1925

Monic Frahn, Hendrik Johannsen (Modellbau)
Timo Riechert, Markus Schedensack, Jörg Weber
(Zeichnungen)

Walter Gropius
Meisterhaus Feininger
Dessau, 1926

Stefan Moser, Ronny Neitsch (Modellbau)
Anke Becker, Manuela Krusch, Stefan Moser
(Zeichnungen)

Hans Scharoun
Haus 33, Weißenhofsiedlung
Stuttgart, 1927

Robert Bleschert, Karin Doberstau, Antje Uebernickel
(Modellbau und Zeichnungen)

Theo van Doesburg
Café de l'Aubette
Straßburg, 1928

Christoph Messow, Anja Schirrmeister (Modellbau)
Sandra Bernhardt, Yvonne Erward, Karsten Hönig
(Zeichnungen)

Ludwig Mies van der Rohe
Barcelona-Pavillon
Barcelona 1929

Andreas Gernandt, Hagen Rust (Modellbau)
Daniela Siede (Zeichnungen)

Le Corbusier
Villa Savoye
Poissy, 1931

*Jochen Kretschmer, Anja Kramski,
Georgia Martinelli* (Modellbau)
Stafan Fast (Zeichnungen)

Frank Lloyd Wright
Haus E. J. Kaufmann, Fallingwater
Mill Run, 1939

Martin Riechel, Toralf Sontag
(Modellbau und Zeichnungen)

Charles & Ray Eames
Eames House
Pacific Palisades, Los Angeles, 1949

*Sebastian Bähring, Bernd Kolbe, Sabine Steinert,
Emanuela Tajolini* (Modellbau und Zeichnungen)

Le Corbusier
Chapelle Notre-Dame-du-Haut
Ronchamp, 1954

Martin Edelmann, Lasse Lutjens
(Modellbau und Zeichnungen)

Carlo Scarpa
Olivetti Showroom
Venedig, 1958

Julian Reisenberger (Modellbau und Zeichnungen)

Robert Venturi
Haus für Vanna Venturi
Chestnut Hill, 1964

Andrea Keller (Modellbau)
Bettina Hein (Zeichnungen)

Hermann Hertzberger
Centraal Beheer
Apeldoorn, 1972

Anke Ponert, Nicole Ritzrau, Annekatrin Thomas
(Modellbau und Zeichnungen)

Mario Botta
Casa Bianchi
Riva San Vitale, 1973

Andrea Gernand, Hagen Rust (Modellbau)
Daniel Reich (Zeichnungen)

Mario Campi, Franco Pessina
Casa Felder
Lugano, 1973

Monica Pytlik (Modellbau und Zeichnungen)

Louis I. Kahn
Yale Center for British Art,
New Haven, 1977

*Gesine Nagel, Frank Pfefferlein, Konrad Scheibe,
Lorenzo Moneta* (Modellbau und Zeichnungen)

Tadao Ando
Haus Koshino
Ashiya, 1981

Bagrikova, Jung, Meinecke (Modellbau)
Cornelia Becker, Christian Bodack (Zeichnungen)

Christian de Portzamparc
Café Beaubourg
Paris, 1986

Tilmann Schäufele (Modellbau)
Matthias Seidel, Nora Steinhöfel (Zeichnungen)

Günther Domenig Steinhaus Steindorf, 1986	*Frank Aßmann, Petra Netz* (Modellbau und Zeichnungen)	Betreuung Prof. Dr.-Ing. habil. Egon Schirmbeck Dipl.-Ing. Dipl.-Formgest. Jochen Burhenne Dipl.-Ing. Christiane Ern

Günther Domenig
Steinhaus
Steindorf, 1986

Frank Aßmann, Petra Netz
(Modellbau und Zeichnungen)

Eduardo Samsó
Nick Havanna Disco
Barcelona, 1986

*Ruth Höppner, Arne Schemmerling,
Katrin Voigtländer*
(Zeichnungen)

Zaha Hadid
Werksfeuerwehr
Weil am Rhein, 1993

Andreas Heym (Modellbau)
Stefan Müller, Anja Werzner (Zeichnungen)

Peter Zumthor
Therme Vals
Vals, 1996

Michael Niehaus, Christian Schmidt, Ricardo Santos
(Modellbau)
Gunnar Stendel, Antje Wunderlich (Zeichnungen)

UNStudio van Berkel & Bos
Möbius-Haus
Het Gooi, 1998

Stefan Moser, Ronny Neitsch (Modellbau)
Anke Becker, Manuela Krusch, Stefan Moser
(Zeichnungen)

Axel Schultes, Charlotte Frank
Krematorium
Berlin, 1998

Bernd Much, Volker Zimmermann (Modellbau)
Ricardo Santos (Zeichnungen)

Rem Koolhaas
Maison à Bordeaux
Bordeaux, 1998

Oliver Droop (Modellbau)
Markus Bischoff, Ulf Steinbrecher (Zeichnungen)

William Alsop
Peckham Library
London, 1999

Stefanie Helmke, Kathrin Nitschke, Wiebke Vettermann
(Modellbau und Zeichnungen)

Peter Zumthor
Schweizer Pavillon
Hannover, 2000

Li He, Tristan Bohn (Modellbau)
Robert Grimm (Zeichnungen)

Frank O. Gehry
DZ Bank AG
Berlin, 2001

Florian Reuter, Ina Mergen
(Modellbau und Zeichnungen)

Betreuung
Prof. Dr.-Ing. habil. Egon Schirmbeck
Dipl.-Ing. Dipl.-Formgest. Jochen Burhenne
Dipl.-Ing. Christiane Ern
Dr.-Ing. Hans Jürgen Katzig
Dipl.-Ing. Barbara Klinghammer
Dipl.-Ing. Dipl.-Des. Jons Messedat
Dipl.-Ing. Ursula Steinert
Dipl.-Ing. Günter Weber
Dipl.-Ing. Kerstin Hohm
Dipl.-Ing. Ulrike Altenmüller
Dipl.-Ing. Natascha Grap
Dr.-Ing. Christian Hanke
Dipl.-Ing. Till Boettger

Betreuung Modellbau
Bodo Steger
Martin Edelmann
Maria Thieme
Ringo Gunkel

Index

Frank Lloyd Wright Unity Temple Chicago, 1907	*Eckhard Breilmann* (model) *Oliver Burk, Matthias Gühne* (drawings)	Frank Lloyd Wright E. J. Kaufmann House, Fallingwater Mill Run, 1939	*Martin Riechel, Toralf Sontag* (model and drawings)
Frank Lloyd Wright Frederick C. Robie House Chicago, 1910	*Mario Anschütz, Ilka Hausmann, Michael Rohner, Sandra Wiedemann* (model and drawings)	Charles & Ray Eames Eames House Pacific Palisades, Los Angeles, 1949	*Sebastian Bähring, Bernd Kolbe, Sabine Steinert, Emanuela Tajolini* (model and drawings)
Robert van 't Hoff Villa Henny Utrecht, 1919	*Sabrina Colombo, Loris Negro* (model) *Claudia Lübbe* (drawings)	Le Corbusier Chapelle Notre-Dame-du-Haut Ronchamp, 1954	*Martin Edelmann, Lasse Lutjens* (model and drawings)
Theo van Doesburg, Cornelis van Eesteren Maison Particulière Paris, 1923	*Jonas Jüttner, Jan Schneidewind* (model and drawings)	Carlo Scarpa Olivetti Showroom Venice, 1958	*Julian Reisenberger* (model and drawings)
Gerrit T. Rietveld Schroeder House Utrecht, 1924	*Julia Brinkmann, Sabine Kamke, Arne Mailbohm* (model) *Virginijus Gerdvilis* (drawings)	Robert Venturi House for Vanna Venturi Chestnut Hill, 1964	*Andrea Keller* (model) *Bettina Hein* (drawings)
Le Corbusier Pavillon de L'Esprit Nouveau Paris, 1925	*Monic Frahn, Hendrik Johannsen* (model) *Timo Riechert, Markus Schedensack, Jörg Weber* (drawings)	Herman Hertzberger Centraal Beheer Apeldoorn, 1972	*Anke Ponert, Nicole Ritzrau, Annekatrin Thomas* (model and drawings)
Walter Gropius Meisterhaus Feininger Dessau, 1926	*Stefan Moser, Ronny Neitsch* (model) *Anke Becker, Manuela Krusch, Stefan Moser* (drawings)	Mario Botta Casa Bianchi Riva San Vitale, 1973	*Andrea Gernand, Hagen Rust* (model) *Daniel Reich* (drawings)
Hans Scharoun House 33, Weißenhofsiedlung Stuttgart, 1927	*Robert Bleschert, Karin Doberstau, Antje Uebernickel* (model and drawings)	Mario Campi, Franco Pessina Casa Felder Lugano, 1973	*Monica Pytlik* (model and drawings)
Theo van Doesburg Café de l'Aubette Strasbourg, 1928	*Christoph Messow, Anja Schirrmeister* (model) *Sandra Bernhardt, Yvonne Erward, Karsten Hönig* (drawings)	Louis I. Kahn Yale Center for British Art, New Haven, 1977	*Gesine Nagel, Frank Pfefferlein, Konrad Scheibe, Lorenzo Moneta* (model and drawings)
Ludwig Mies van der Rohe Barcelona-Pavillon Barcelona 1929	*Andreas Gernandt, Hagen Rust* (model) *Daniela Siede* (drawings)	Tadao Ando Koshino House Ashiya, 1981	*Bagrikova, Jung, Meinecke* (model) *Cornelia Becker, Christian Bodack* (drawings)
Le Corbusier Villa Savoye Poissy, 1931	*Jochen Kretschmer, Anja Kramski, Georgia Martinelli* (model) *Stafan Fast* (drawings)	Christian de Portzamparc Café Beaubourg Paris, 1986	*Tilmann Schäufele* (model) *Matthias Seidel, Nora Steinhöfel* (drawings)

WIR SETZEN MASSSTÄBE

Seit mehr als 110 Jahren realisiert Züblin erfolgreich anspruchsvolle Bauprojekte im In- und Ausland und ist im deutschen Hoch- und Ingenieurbau die Nummer eins. Wir bieten unseren Kunden ein umfassendes Leistungsspektrum und entwickeln maßgeschneiderte Lösungen für technisch und wirtschaftlich optimierte Bauvorhaben jeder Art und Größe. Das Know-how und die Innovationskraft unserer rund 12.000 Mitarbeiter sind dabei die Basis unseres Erfolgs. Ob im Ingenieur- oder Brückenbau, im komplexen Schlüsselfertigbau, Tunnelbau oder im Bereich Public Private Partnership – Züblin setzt Maßstäbe.

Ed. Züblin AG
Direktion Mitte, Bereich Thüringen
Fischergasse 10, 07743 Jena
Tel. +49 3641 591-3
Fax +49 3641 591-400
mitte-jena@zueblin.de

Individuell formbar.

Knauf Falt- und Biegetechnik.

Knauf Platten sind individuell formbar. Nach Wunsch vorgefertigt, als Formteilelemente oder fertig geleimt lieferbar. Das Ergebnis: präzise Ausführung nach individuellen Vorgaben – für perfekte Gestaltung an Decke und Wand.

Formteile sicher planen **www.knauf-formbar.de**

ENTWÄSSERUNG IN BESTFORM **BIRCO**

GALABAU
DESIGN

Klassik trifft Moderne.

Im Zentrum von Münster setzen der Neubau der NRW.BANK und die Sanierung des benachbarten, denkmalgeschützten Gebäudes übergreifende architektonische Akzente.

BIRCO gestaltete die Platz- und Fassadenentwässerung mit 10 verschiedenen Objektrinnen in einem ganzheitlichen System. Modernes Design und optimale Funktionalität nach Maß verbunden.

www.birco.de

Günther Domenig Steinhaus Steindorf, 1986	*Frank Aßmann, Petra Netz* (model and drawings)	*Assistance* *Prof. Dr.-Ing. habil. Egon Schirmbeck* *Dipl.-Ing. Dipl.-Formgest. Jochen Burhenne* *Dipl.-Ing. Christiane Ern*
Eduardo Samsó Nick Havanna Disco Barcelona, 1986	*Ruth Höppner, Arne Schemmerling,* *Katrin Voigtländer* (drawings)	*Dr.-Ing. Hans Jürgen Katzig* *Dipl.-Ing. Barbara Klinghammer* *Dipl.-Ing. Dipl.-Des. Jons Messedat* *Dipl.-Ing. Ursula Steinert*
Zaha Hadid Vitra Fire Station Weil am Rhein, 1993	*Andreas Heym* (model) *Stefan Müller, Anja Werzner* (drawings)	*Dipl.-Ing. Günter Weber* *Dipl.-Ing. Kerstin Hohm* *Dipl.-Ing. Ulrike Altenmüller* *Dipl.-Ing. Natascha Grap*
Peter Zumthor Therme Vals Vals, 1996	*Michael Niehaus, Christian Schmidt,* *Ricardo Santos* (model) *Gunnar Stendel, Antje Wunderlich* (drawings)	*Dr.-Ing. Christian Hanke* *Dipl.-Ing. Till Boettger*
UNStudio van Berkel & Bos Moebius House Het Gooi, 1998	*Stefan Moser, Ronny Neitsch* (model) *Anke Becker, Manuela Krusch, Stefan Moser* (drawings)	*Assistance with model building* *Bodo Steger* *Martin Edelmann* *Maria Thieme*
Axel Schultes, Charlotte Frank Krematorium Berlin, 1998	*Bernd Much, Volker Zimmermann* (model) *Ricardo Santos* (drawings)	*Ringo Gunkel*
Rem Koolhaas Maison à Bordeaux Bordeaux, 1998	*Oliver Droop* (model) *Markus Bischoff, Ulf Steinbrecher* (drawings)	
William Alsop Peckham Library London, 1999	*Stefanie Helmke, Kathrin Nitschke, Wiebke Vettermann* (model and drawings)	
Peter Zumthor Schweizer Pavillon Hanover, 2000	*Li He, Tristan Bohn* (model) *Robert Grimm* (drawings)	
Frank O. Gehry DZ Bank AG Berlin, 2001	*Florian Reuter, Ina Mergen* (model and drawings)	

Armstrong

Durch eine umfangreiche und technisch innovative Produktpalette bietet Armstrong immer die perfekte Bodenlösung:

- DLW Linoleum
- DLW Vinyl
- DLW Luxury Vinyl
- DLW Nadelvlies

Lassen Sie sich inspirieren von einer erstaunlichen Fülle an Farben, Strukturen und Materialien.

Mehr erfahren Sie unter **www.armstrong.de**

BODENBELÄGE

Die *Deutsche Nationalbibliothek* verzeichnet diese Publikation in der *Deutschen Nationalbibliografie;* detaillierte bibliografische Daten sind im Internet über *http://dnb.d-nb.de* abrufbar. The *Deutsche Bibliothek* lists this publication in the *Deutsche Nationalbibliografie*. Detailed bibliographical data available on the internet at *http://dnb.ddb.de*.

ISBN 978-3-86922-179-3 (deutsche Ausgabe)
ISBN 978-3-86922-180-9 (English edition)

© 2011 by *DOM publishers*, Berlin
www.dom-publishers.com

Dieses Werk ist urheberrechtlich geschützt. Jede Verwendung außerhalb der Grenzen des Urheberrechtsgesetzes ist ohne Zustimmung des Verlags unzulässig und strafbar. Dies gilt insbesondere für Vervielfältigungen, Übersetzungen, Mikroverfilmungen sowie die Einspeicherung und Verarbeitung in elektronischen Systemen. Die Nennung der Quellen und Urheber erfolgt nach bestem Wissen und Gewissen. This work is subject to copyright. All rights reserved. No part of this publication may be reproduced, stored in a retrieval system, or transferred, in any form or by any means, electronic, mechanical, photocopying, recording, or otherwise, without the prior written permission of the publishers. Sources and owners of rights are stated to the best of our knowledge; please signal any we might have omitted.

Redaktion Editing	Till Boettger
Übersetzung Translation	The Missing Link English Studio (American English)
Lektorat Proofreading	Mandy Kasek
Gestaltung Graphic Design	Till Boettger, Sophie Gläser
Druck Printed by	Tiger Printing (Hong Kong) Co. Ltd., China
Gefördert von Supported by	Armstrong DLW GmbH BIRCO Baustoffwerk GmbH Ed. Züblin AG, Direktion Mitte, Bereich Thüringen Knauf Gips KG
Fotonachweis Photo Credits	William Alsop, Peckham Library; Le Corbusier, Wallfahrtskapelle Ronchamp; Frank O. Gehry, DZ Bank; Peter Zumthor, Schweizer Pavillon: Fotos von Thomas Gehnke und Ulf Ströde. Alle anderen Fotos wurden von Christian Hanke und Timo Riechert zur Verfügung gestellt. William Alsop, Peckham Library; Le Corbusier, Wallfahrtskapelle Ronchamp; Frank O. Gehry, DZ Bank; Peter Zumthor, Schweizer Pavillon: Images by Thomas Gehnke and Ulf Ströde. Other images courtesy of Christian Hanke and Timo Riechert.